Secret Child

Secret Child

Nancy Moore

Pickering Paperbacks

Copyright © 1986 by Nancy Moore

First Published in 1986
by Pickering & Inglis,
Marshall Pickering
3 Beggarwood Lane,
Basingstoke, Hants RG23 7LP,
United Kingdom
A subsidiary of the Zondervan Corporation Inc.

British Library Cataloguing in Publication Data

Moore, Nancy
  Secret child.
  1. Birth parents—Identification
  I. Title
  362.7'34'0924   HV875

  ISBN 0–7208–0681–X

Phototypeset in Linotron Plantin
by Input Typesetting Ltd, London

Printed and bound in Great Britain by
Hazell Watson & Viney Ltd, Aylesbury, Bucks.

In Dedication. . .
. . . to the One who can keep (me) from falling and set (me) in the presence of His glory, jubilant and above reproach, to the Only God our Saviour, be glory and majesty, might and authority through Jesus Christ our Lord. . . Jude 25.

And with gratefulness for. . .
Eric, my beloved husband and best friend, who has loved me through it all.
Andrew and Jean, our two children, ever a source of wonder and a joy to have around.
Tom, a special gift from the Lord, who was given back and who brought the delight of JoAnne, Joshua and Troy into our lives.
Glen and Nita Rye, Tom's parents; God's answer in my time of need.

I acknowledge . . .

. . . without Eric's help and encouragement this would never have been completed.

. . . Edward England's skill and direction which enabled me to see this to completion.

. . . others who read over the manuscript and gave sound advice; Mike, Kathryn, Molly, Helen, Pattie and especially Valerie.

Contents

Psalm 71

You shall ever be the theme of my praise.

Although I have not the skill of a poet
I will begin with a tale of great deeds, O Lord God
and sing (tell) of thy righteousness, thine alone.

. . . Thou hast done great things,
Who is like thee, O God?

Thou hast made me pass through bitter and deep
distress,
yet dost revive me once again.

. . . songs of joy shall be on my lips.

Introduction

'Oh, you should write a book about all that God has done in your life.'

Variations of that statement came to me at least a dozen times in the months following my reunion with Tom. Each time I brushed aside the idea with hardly a thought; I hated any writing and my low university English composition marks showed my great weakness in this area.

But after hearing this refrain so often I did say, 'Lord, if you want it done make it clear to me.' I was reluctantly willing but was completely sure I would never write.

A couple of months later I received a letter from Edward England, a literary agent. He asked if I would write my story. I felt frightened at the thought of doing it but realized that this was from the Lord and I must do it. Thus began many months of writing in the midst of working almost full-time.

My husband, Eric, has been a tremendous help and a patient corrector of innumerable mistakes and has helped me put on paper this story, God's story, of His love and restoration.

1: Deserted

We had all strayed like sheep
each of us had gone his own way,
but the Lord laid upon Him (Jesus)
the guilt of us all.
Isaiah 53:6

For I know the plans I have for you says the Lord.
They are plans for good and not for evil,
to give you a future and a hope.
In those days when you pray I will listen.
You will find me, if you look for Me in earnest.
Jeremiah 29:11–14 (Living Bible)

Thou it was who didst fashion my inward parts;
thou didst knit me together in my mother's womb.
Psalm 139:13

'You are pregnant.' The doctor's words, though spoken kindly, were like a slap in the face and they confirmed my gravest suspicions. I had gone to him expecting the worst and now I knew it was true. I felt completely numb and sat there in his office, immobile. Terror rose up in me. This couldn't be. What was I to do? Where could I turn?

I was not yet 18 years old, living in a small town in Minnesota. My eagerly awaited nurse's training was to start in a few months, and would fulfil an ambition I had cherished for as long as I could remember.

Life was busy and interesting; life was fun. I didn't

have problems at home and my parents were kind and loving.

Now my life was shattered and lying in pieces and I realized I didn't know how to pick them up and put them back together. What could I do? There was no one to talk to; no one that I dared share this with and I wept as my fears crystallized before me into a terrible reality. I knew it would be a crushing blow to my parents and they must not be told. They must be spared. I wanted to shield them from unnecessary hurt. My mother in particular had had some very painful experiences over the years and I didn't want to add to them.

How had I got into this situation, which now threatened my entire future? We had moved to this town just a year before and since then I'd made many friends and was involved not only in school activities but also in those at church. Like many others I had a part-time job after school.

Soon after our move I met and began to date one of the fellows, who seemed to be pleasant enough, involved with the activities I enjoyed. We became increasingly serious about each other and I cared deeply for him.

Under great emotional pressure I found myself a reluctant partner in sin. Now I was having to bear the consequences of my sin, and another's. I believed sex outside of marriage wasn't right; so where did I go wrong? I wasn't perfect and yet had not set out to live this way. Was I just searching for real love and affection and unable to resist a counterfeit of it?

I had, somehow, to go on living in the midst of my world falling apart, but how could I carry on in this appalling mess?

What was to be done first? I went immediately to tell my boyfriend but even as I prepared to meet him I felt afraid. Did I sense what his reaction would be? Upon hearing that I was pregnant he left me and to make it more definite, he left town. The pain of betrayal cut deep. I had been used and discarded.

Somehow I felt I couldn't inflict the shameful news

upon my parents. I desperately wanted to say something, to share this burden with them but could not. It was so terrible and my lips seemed to be sealed. I was unable to tell them of my pregnancy. And since I had only lived in the town for a year I didn't feel close enough to my girl friends to say anything to them and, of course, couldn't trust them not to tell anyone. If they did tell anyone it would certainly find its way back to my parents. I knew the pain this would inflict and wanted to protect them. I was alone in this and somehow had to get through it without outside help, so I stubbornly refused to admit defeat.

I turned inward and bottled up my feelings of rejection, hurt and utter helplessness. My heart broke, bit by bit, as each day brought with it the deepening realization of how huge my problem was. I longed to know what to do, but the only ones who could help me, my parents, had to be protected at all costs from the shame of this, I thought.

The disgrace of an out-of-wedlock pregnancy in 1956, was still immense and I felt the full weight of society's condemnation of someone 'in trouble', as the saying then was. The future for a child, born to and cared for, by an unmarried girl was not easy; such a child would carry a stigma and face rejection, disapproval and scorn. My heart ached with all of this. I did not want my child to have this inflicted on him so there was no way to keep my child under these circumstances. I was overwhelmed by this social, financial and emotional pressure. There was no way to support a child on my own nor offer any hope of a normal life.

Should I get an abortion? That would get me out of the mess my life was in. The decisions were mine alone to make. There was no one I felt able to turn to for help or advice. Would an abortion really solve my problem? Could I get one? Where?

Some girls had them but it certainly was very uncommon then. I didn't know where to go to have this done, couldn't ask, and deep down really knew I could not go through with it. I could not kill this life within me; this was my baby and I couldn't snuff out its life.* But what else could be done? How could I go on like this?

I walked those days in crushing loneliness with no one to pour out my troubles to. Maybe, I thought, if I didn't think about being pregnant then it would all disappear. It just couldn't be real; this couldn't be happening to me. I felt dazed, in a nightmare. No one in our family had been pregnant and unmarried. The shame of it all was an overwhelming weight upon me. I couldn't bear to think about it and so it was suppressed; I ignored it all and hoped it would go away.

Perhaps this way of dealing with things on my own could be traced far back to my childhood. My own home was broken when my father left my mother and me shortly after my first birthday. I became aware when growing up that this rejection was a heavy weight my mother carried over the years along with other emotional wounds. When our home broke up she returned to university for a while and then worked full-time to support us and so from a young age I was often under the care of a number of different people.

One of them who cared so lovingly for me was my father's sister who looked after me for several months at a time and who came to think of me as her own daughter. She remained very dear to us as a family. Even when back with my mother I was still in the care of others for long periods and therefore not with her very much.

There was really no one to trust my confidences to or to share with and so, in many respects, I was on my own emotionally. This caused me to be very independent, out of necessity, but strangely still sociable. Through all of this I learned to cope with my feelings and difficulties all on my own. Perhaps it was over these years I also learned to repress them, when they were too difficult to bear as I knew no other way to handle them.

Surprisingly I turned out fairly normal. (At least some people think so!) This was undoubtedly due to a good mother and others who cared for me in the best way they could. But through all this came the ability, out of necessity, to deal with my emotions on my own, rarely sharing my feelings with others.

When I was six my mother remarried. My step-father was a kind, thoughtful man who formally adopted me just a year later.

Three years passed and then I had a new baby brother and at the age of nine, I was old enough to really enjoy him and to help with his care. My parents gave me consistent love and discipline but we were never close emotionally. Was there a part of me looking for real intimacy? I wanted someone to share my deepest feelings with.

Once more the familiar pattern of repressing my feelings emerged as I faced the most difficult circumstances of my life. I denied my boyfriend's rejection and attempted to escape the situation; it made me want to run but where could I go? I denied the problem, pushed it down and didn't think about it. There settled over me a terrible black numbness of spirit. I was trapped with no way to escape.

This school year must be finished, that I knew, so I maintained all my usual activities, school work and student council activities, as one of its officers. Underneath all this activity no one knew the distress I felt; no one knew what I was going through.

I cried inside, a silent weeping, but only rarely did I allow myself to shed any tears. Bottle it up and shove it down. This was the only way to cope with such an overpowering feeling of utter helplessness.

The nights were long, too long, there was too much to think about. The uncertainties were enormous; what was I to do? Things were out of my control. Which way could I turn? I was trapped, encased in a leaden suit of distress and fear. It grew tighter every day. I hid my real feelings of desperation from everyone. Outwardly I was my usual self, but inside the burden of heartache and fear grew heavier.

Where was God? I knew He existed and I prayed on occasions but knew He certainly wouldn't want to be bothered with this situation. He would not be pleased with me; I had done wrong. I had involved myself in this so I must get myself through it somehow.

Towards the end of the school year things became even more hectic for those of us who were graduating in early June. I had been accepted into the school of nursing which began early in September and so just stubbornly ploughed ahead, determined that I had to keep on somehow. If I stopped and admitted defeat I would come apart emotionally. My body was showing changes but not enough to offer people a confirmation of my pregnancy. Perhaps they were suspicious but I carried on as though everything was normal. Graduation day came and the gowns we all wore covered my shape when I had to go up on the stage, in front of everyone, to receive my scholarship for nurses training.

The next week I went away to a large city some distance from my home town. I had accepted a job there with a family helping with the cooking and light housework. This job was a life saver as I could be away from everyone I knew. My baby was due to be born in less than three months.

The people I worked for were a warm hearted couple and the work suited me. Life wasn't too strenuous in their home beside a lovely lake. This beautiful and peaceful setting was a real haven of calm and quiet for me. Did they suspect my condition? I don't know. But no one spoke of it and they seemed pleased with my work.

One night, lying in bed listening to the storm and the rain beat on the roof, I realized the full extent of the terrible mess I was in. I was desperate and cried out to God; a God I knew about, being a churchgoer, and yet didn't really know in a personal way. But I knew enough however, to bargain with Him.

'God, just get me through this and I'll follow You.'*

I was starting to understand that He was the only one

16

who could do anything for me. Yet He seemed so distant, so far away. Did He really care about me? It didn't seem possible.

A few weeks later I realized that my pregnancy could no longer be ignored and I must get to a doctor as I had not been to one for so long. It had been many months since the doctor at home had first told me the shocking news. Tests were undertaken and I was recalled a week later for more.

'You are very ill,' the doctor told me gently. 'The tests indicate you have toxaemia. In order to treat it and reduce your abnormally high blood pressure you must be hospitalized immediately.'

Once again a doctor's words stunned me. What did this mean? How sick was I? Was my baby all right? It made me more frightened than ever. I went back and told the couple I worked for that I had a kidney condition and the doctor was admitting me to hospital right away.

Just a few days previously, the doctor had sent me to see a social worker to discuss my future and that of my baby. My recollections of our meeting are extremely vague. Was that due to the amnesia which is apparently very common among girls having to give up their babies? Is it the only way one can cope with the pain of such a situation?

I was admitted to hospital and sedated heavily. The doctors were trying to stabilise my condition and get my blood pressure down and under control. They told me if they didn't do so there was the possibility I could have convulsions or other complications. They gave me so much medication I had to be wakened for meals and helped to eat.

This went on for several days; days which are almost a total blank. I was too ill and too heavily sedated to be aware of much. Thankfully this spared me from being more aware of the anguish I felt. I felt utterly helpless, stripped of all hope and already grieving for my child.

I cried when the woman in the bed next to me had her baby with her; distraught because there was no way

I could keep mine. I couldn't care for my child and this crushed me.

Labour began and it seemed to go on for ever. Morphine was given to sedate me still further. I felt so alone. No one stayed with me to comfort or hold my hand and help me get through this.

Suddenly, in the middle of labour, my parents appeared. The couple I'd worked for were concerned and found out from the hospital what was happening and called my parents to see if they knew.

The encounter with them was brief and I was in a haze of medication, pain and distress. It shocked me to see them suddenly appear and I was unable to say much except, 'I'm sorry, I didn't want you to know. I didn't want to hurt you.'

I wept realizing just how hard it was for them also. They did not condemn me and I sensed their concern as they tried to comfort me but I was too ill to be able to respond. They were only allowed to stay a brief time, then they had to leave and again there was no one to be with me. The tears and pain came in a flood as I lay there fighting panic.*

Shortly afterwards my son was born. The nurse held him up for me to see.

'He's a beautiful baby boy. Just perfect.'

My eyes didn't seem to want to focus. Was he really all right? I could hardly tell. The heavy medication and the long hours of labour had taken their toll, I was numb. I pulled down the shutters of my heart.

My baby was taken away and I must have finally succumbed to the sedation and remembered nothing more. He was gone.

My child was gone. A part of me died that day and lay like a cold, ugly stone, heavy upon my heart.

It sank home more fully over the next few days with growing pain; I couldn't keep my own child. He could not remain with me; I could not hope to care for a child on my own and I did not want him to grow up without a father. He must be given the chance of a good home and loving parents. Somehow, with what knowledge I had of God, I prayed.

'Lord, please, please take care of him. He's yours Lord. See that he has a good home.'

To allow my son's adoption was the most difficult decision I ever made. It was a decision of love but it broke my heart.

A few days later I was discharged from the hospital to stay in an aftercare home before going back to my family. My one enduring memory of this whole time is of leaving the hospital. The scene is branded with tears deep in my heart, and remains as vivid today as when it first happened.

I walked out of the hospital down a long hallway, alone. It seemed to stretch out without ending; ahead of me walked a social worker, she was holding my baby. He was all bundled up and I couldn't get a glimpse of him. It was the longest walk of my life. We were both taken in the same car to the home; the social worker and my baby in the back seat and I in the front. We were both crying. It was the last time I would be with him but even then I was unable to see his face.

After a few days spent recovering I returned home to my parents. I was broken. My child was no longer mine. He would never know how hard it had been for me to relinquish him. If only he could know I loved him enough to give him a future but I would never know what had become of him.

I was in a state of shock and spent most of my time sleeping. I was aware of the distress of my parents over the situation but we didn't talk about it. A wall of silence came down around this whole episode. We never really spoke about it. They tried to help me recover and were kind and tender towards me as I attempted to pick up the pieces. After a few short days I left home and began my nurse's training. Somehow I had to go on with life.

2: Life Has To Go On

Comfort, comfort, my people –
it is the voice of your God.
Speak tenderly to Jerusalem
and tell her this,
that she has fulfilled her term of bondage,
that her penalty is paid.
Isaiah 40:1–2

. . . but Christ died for us while we were yet sinners
and that is God's own proof of His love towards us.
Romans 5:8

'Life has to go on.' How often had I heard that saying
and now I realized the truth of it. I had to go on living
in spite of my grief.

The milestone following so close after the birth of my
child was the beginning of nurses' training. This was a
desire cherished since childhood and yet I had come so
close to being unable to fulfil it. Now it was a longing
muted by the trauma of the past months but it kept me
focused on something other than my inner anguish.

September 4th: up the flight of wide granite steps and
through the huge front door of the nurses' dormitory I
went. Here, at Northwestern Hospital in Minneapolis, I
would spend the next three years. We were welcomed
and assigned to a room, with a new room-mate for the
coming year. Outwardly, I was like the rest of my classmates – happy go lucky. Inwardly, things were drasti-
cally different.

Just over two weeks before my baby had been born.

For my survival all the recent events were suppressed deep in my memory. Of course nothing was forgotten; it was still there unresolved and merely out of my daily consciousness.

At times every painful detail would surface to torment me. I was living in shock, a state of semi-amnesia, and mercifully being numbed to a lot of the hurt. My emotions were blunted, grief was lessened but so was joy. This denial of the agony was necessary. It allowed me to hold myself together and be able to cope with life. The necessity of following the daily routine kept me functioning and slowly mending.

This was where I wanted to be and longed to do well. But was it possible? I felt so absolutely exhausted and drained both physically and emotionally.

Those early days were filled with many new things; dormitory life and getting acquainted with my roommate, Myra; uniforms to be measured for; and stacks of books crammed with apparently endless, unfamiliar facts, formulae and ideas. Could there really be that much to learn and would it be possible to take it in?

The next week we had orientation to the college, where we would have many of our first year academic classes. There, at Macalester's lovely tree-lined campus, we would take many hours of chemistry, anatomy and microbiology classes and the accompanying laboratory work.

Life was busy from the very beginning and in my exhaustion I was frequently forced to find a quiet corner and go to sleep. I slept, even while on my feet, during some of our nursing arts practical classes as we stood around a bedside and watched demonstrations. Gradually, I did become stronger and entered into many activities with my classmates, yet no-one was aware of anything amiss in my life.

Clinical classes were interesting as we learned practical nursing skills, although it was not particularly thrilling to learn how to make a bed with proper 'hospital corners'. We enjoyed lots of fun and laughter, learning to give injections by following the common method of using oranges for practice. Their texture is supposed to resemble that of flesh!

When we became proficient enough we were allowed to try our skills on each other and finally on real patients. There were many fascinating things to absorb as we learned to carry out increasingly complex tasks.

But I felt almost paralysed when encountering classes in which there was any memorising to do. Remembering relevant facts from these classes when, at the same time, I was trying to forget traumatic events, was extremely difficult. The suppression of my grief caused great difficulty in doing any of this memory work.

My child, my child where are you?

This question came to mind at intervals but I knew I should not think about him.* Life should go on as though nothing has happened. Everything was normal; I was all right; or so I thought. How foolish I was.

There were seventy five of us in that freshman class and several became close friends. We enjoyed good times together but even with those closest to me I could not share everything. Somehow I felt those deep hurts were mine to carry alone.

'Come on, let's go out for a bite to eat,' was often the cry that echoed down the dormitory hall. Nurses are always hungry! If we weren't eating we would probably be thinking about doing so. Later that year, as I gained strength, I began to work occasional evenings helping a catering firm. This enabled me to earn spending money and enjoy even more good food – free!

Early that first autumn in training, I was invited by my room-mate and other friends to attend a Bible Study which was held in our dormitory. A lady came in to lead this each week and it was fascinating. This was the first time that I had seriously studied the Bible for myself.

My heart was receptive and I listened with new ears to things which I must have heard at church for years. The realization came, I needed Christ. My heart had been thoroughly prepared by the events of the past year and it was ready for this planting of the Seed.

My strong self-will had been broken, and my eyes were wide open to see that I personally needed to respond to what the Lord had done. It was necessary to do more than just see my need; that I had seen for some time.

It became clear just how independent and wilful I really was; all my life I had gone my own way and done what was right in my own eyes. Now I saw Jesus was showing me that my selfishness was what He called sin. The conviction came that for this He had come and for this He had died. It was for ME He died. How could I have been blind to this before? There was a real drawing of my heart towards the Lord.*

It was only a couple of months ago that I came into nursing with merely a head knowledge of this. Now I wanted to know Jesus personally, like my friends. Exactly when I crossed this bridge to real life, to eternal life, wasn't clear but I knew I had done so.

My heart began to soften and unfold as I felt the great love that God had for me – personally – as He allowed His only Son to die on my behalf. Sensing this love I could no longer remain indifferent or it would be deliberate rejection.

Christ loved and died for me as I was, a sinner going my own way. I had nothing to offer, just a tired, messed up life. He gave Himself for me and I wanted to give Him my life in return; to give Him my love in response to His great love for me. I did this. Then He was able to take on Himself my sinful nature and declare me forgiven in God's sight; not for my being good or doing anything but because I accepted that which He had ALREADY done.*

Jesus wrapped me in HIS righteousness.

There was no need to strive to be good enough. Jesus set me free. Whatever good I had tried to do before to earn God's favour was like 'filthy rags' in His sight. Now He put on me His robes of righteousness. I was clean, forgiven and released because of what He had done on my behalf.

How long had the Lord been standing knocking at the door of my life, wanting and needing to be invited in? How long had I seen Him but did not know He needed my permission to enter my life and touch it. How long had the hunger been there and I didn't recognize it for what it was? That void in my life was one that only He could fill. Unsuccessfully, I tried to fill my life with activities and love from others and hadn't allowed Jesus in, so I remained unsatisfied and empty deep down inside myself.

What a sense of peace and freedom this simple act brought, just to turn my life over to His care and control. These things came into focus during the period of a few months. By that Easter, for the first time I really did know that JESUS WAS ALIVE and He had brought me into His family. He gave me that inner confidence and I was experiencing the liberating joy of knowing His total forgiveness and His deep love.

I still wasn't sure how to give Him all those deep wounds and the grief of the past year. I tried to turn them over to Him and knew He understood and would help me to bear them. He began to give me real joy – a gentle joy stealing into my heart quietly, unawares.

Thankfully, we were so busy with studies and work in the hospital that there was little time to think deeply about the past. Instead I tried to forget it in order to stop the inner pain and just concentrated on doing well.

Soon after this, when at home visiting my parents one weekend, I was out shopping and saw my former boyfriend. This was the first time I had seen him since he had walked out of my life more than a year before. Somehow over the past few months the Lord had, unknown to me, done such a work in my life that I did not feel any distress at seeing the man who had rejected me. In spite of all that had happened I only felt sorry for him.

I went over and told him that my baby, a son, had

been born but I had been forced to put him up for adoption. Since then God had enabled me to forgive him for all that had happened.*

He listened without a word, then turned and walked away. That was the last time I ever saw him but no longer felt hurt by his actions: I was free!

Several of us who were in the Bible Study group became linked with 'Nurses' Christian Fellowship' and we gathered with other nurses from around the city who were also developing a relationship with the living Christ, and facing the same situations as us.

They were a delightful, happy group and we enjoyed lots of fun together. It was with their help that I began to establish a good, solid grounding in Christian living. I felt it was the beginning of an exciting adventure with lots to discover along the way and I found the Christian life, contrary to popular opinion, to be anything but dull!

Our first year was quickly over. We were 'capped', which is to say that we received our proper nurses' caps which symbolized powerfully to us our progress towards becoming fully-fledged nurses. I had made it thus far through my first and most difficult year, keenly aware it was only because of the Lord's help. I was a changed person from when the year began.

Myra and I went to Colorado to a camp led by Inter-varsity Christian Fellowship (IVF) for several weeks holiday. This was at Bear Trap Ranch, tucked away in the Rocky Mountains, high above Colorado Springs. At 9000 feet we were amongst the pines, surrounded by even higher peaks and the air was cool and crisp.

What a wonderful place to come for a rest and to learn about the Lord, especially so after the previous exhausting year. How wonderfully He provides what we need, when we need it!

Those weeks were an enjoyable mixture; trail rides, chuck-wagon breakfasts in a nearby meadow, Bar-B-Q's, hiking, and stimulating speakers each evening. There were many students, like myself, from all over the

United States who had come with a desire to study the Bible in a deeper way.

All too soon, the holiday was over and we were back for our second year of training. Now the proportion of time between our clinical work and theory changed; practical work in the hospital with patients took precedence over that in the classroom. Rotations through the different floors began. The operating theatre came first for me and it was a challenge that demanded all my attention.

It proved an excellent way to see, at first hand, the things we had previously learned in anatomy classes. As we became more proficient we were allowed to 'scrub up' and assist in the operations; I enjoyed this but personally, preferred my patients awake!

My three months' spell in the operating theatre ended and my turn came for corresponding times to be spent on the Surgical, Medical, Paediatric, Orthopaedic and Obstetrics floors. We were kept constantly busy with lectures and demonstrations, learning new procedures, then using these in our work with patients.

Pharmacology, drugs and solutions: grams, minims, drachms, ounces and grains. Help! The calculations involved in such matters were definitely not my cup of tea, but they had to be done, and somehow I did them.

Off-duty hours were full of fun, keeping us balanced and able then to return to work and cope with difficult cases. It was good to be in Minneapolis, the City of Lakes, which offered so many delightful places to enjoy. There was swimming in the summer or skating on those same lakes in winter. If I wasn't out enjoying myself my nose was usually in a book and often it was a cook-book. My love of food was the source of many jokes, I was either reading about it or eating it and somehow not gaining weight.

My life must have seemed normal to those around me during all of this time as I entered into life to the full. My friends introduced me to several fine fellows, who I dated occasionally. They were pleasant company but there was no one that I was particularly fond of although some became very good friends. I often wondered if I would ever find someone to love and trust enough to marry. Despite these times of fun I still grieved and often thought of my child.

My son was now two years old. Where was he? What did he look like? It hurt so much even to think about him. I had given him to the Lord to care for and could only trust he was being well looked after and bringing some family great joy. I would pray for him but tried not to dwell on this for long or the inner anguish would be too great. I schooled myself to forget or I'd not survive, my grief would eat me up.

Those second and third years of training continued busily for we spent considerable time in moving to different hospitals for further specialized training.

Psychiatric work came next for me, at a large mental hospital, where some of the patients had been for up to forty years and little could be done for them. Why had they become ill? What had been the events in their lives with which they had been unable to cope? Seeing them I sensed it could have happened to me. Only the Lord kept me whole.

The work in hospital was enjoyable but, increasingly, I came to see that my interest and abilities lay in the area of patient teaching and disease prevention, not just treating illness. Important too was my desire to travel as part of my work. Public Health Nursing appealed to me but I realized that this necessitated further education. It would mean another three years at university. Could I do it? I wanted to try; I applied and was accepted.

Those last few months in training passed quickly. State Board Exams were looming and a million other things had to be done as well. The past three years had been eventful ones; very difficult but rewarding. New life and joy in the Lord had come and He'd helped me to cope with grief. My mind often went back to those hard times at the beginning; how had I coped with it all?

The last few days were upon us with rounds of celebrations including the party my friends and I gave to honour our mothers. We wanted to thank them for all the help and encouragement they had been to us over the years.

Graduation day came; that evening we had our service in one of the old churches in the city. Soft candlelight and the long line of graduates in white uniforms, each carrying two dozen red roses, made an impressive sight. We each went forward to receive our nursing pin, a small gold star, symbolising so much.

A chapter of my life was closing; it had been hard but it also brought joy. In two weeks' time would come yet another challenge as I started at university. What lay ahead?

3: University Days

> Cease to dwell on days gone by
> and to brood over past history.
>
> Here and now I will do a new thing.
>
> I alone, I am He who for His own sake wipes out your
> transgressions, who will remember your sins no
> more.
> Isaiah 43:18–19, 25
>
> . . . Christ Himself, in Him,
> lie hidden all God's treasures of wisdom and
> knowledge.
> Colossians 2:2

Twenty eight thousand students – the University of Minnesota was huge – fourteen times the population of my home town! I had never been part of such a large group. Would I ever find my way around or make any friends? It was exciting though, adjusting to a new way of life and study. Public Health Nursing was going to require three years of hard study.

To become qualified for this would be a challenge. There was much to learn; studies in disease prevention, child development, communicable disease and health education lay ahead. I did wonder sometimes about the relevance of some classes. German and anthropology, what practical use would they be? My poor memory once again caused problems when trying to learn a new language. I worked so hard at this and yet came so close to failure. Was it because I still had to block out painful memories?

A course in Comparative Religions provided useful information but it was sad to see people groping around trying to find God purely by mental effort. They were looking for abstract truths to satisfy themselves, but such vague concepts are cold comfort compared to knowing the living Lord who loved them personally.

As well as carrying a full academic load I was working about twenty five hours a week in a hospital Emergency Room. I found myself stretched to the limit of my newly acquired nursing skills. What an amazing variety of ways people found to hurt themselves!

Patients came in a steady stream, at all hours of the day and night, with an assortment of cuts, bumps and bruises. Because the hospital was close to several major highways we treated more than our share of seriously injured people from car accidents. Many of the accidents would have been prevented with the use of seat belts and it wasn't long before I bought myself some.

It was often two in the morning before I arrived home and began to write my essays or do other assignments after a busy evening at work. And of course I often dropped asleep over my books!

Occasionally I found time to go out with friends or on a date. Once again, although the fellows I met were pleasant, there was no one especially interesting. Would I ever meet a man to love and commit myself to? At times I felt discouraged and doubted there was anyone.

'Lord, is there no one you have for me? You know how I long for someone to provide a deep stable love; someone kind and tender and who loves you too.'

Fortunately I kept busy and so occupied there wasn't time to dwell on the past but the dark memories remained. The thick mist of grief would gather round me and I had to struggle on through it. Where was my son now? Is he even alive; I would never know.

On my arrival at university I became involved with

IVF. It was vital to make Christian friends and to have their support and the spiritual nourishment to go along with the academic challenges I was facing. Our group was a lively one; we had weekly meetings and small Bible study groups as well as lots of social activity. It was here we made close friendships and had an atmosphere that encouraged discussion. We were taught to dig out the answer to our questions from the Word of God. I learned to lead a study and find principles to apply in making decisions about everyday issues. We often had intense deliberations and were not afraid to question and work through to see what God was saying and what our response should be. My mind was being stretched and my vision enlarged.*

In all of this I came to see that everything and everyone needed to be evaluated in terms of the place they accorded to the person of Christ. Was Jesus absolutely central and magnified as Saviour and Lord?

On our weekend retreats we had time to study things in more depth as well as enjoy times of real hilarity together. It was an amusing, crazy group. It was healing for me to be part of it.

I see, in retrospect, how this was a time of putting down my roots within this caring, stimulating environment and setting the course of my life. I was building my faith on Jesus who would prove to be, in the years ahead, my ultimate foundation and safe dwelling place just as He had promised in His Word.*

It was continuing my search for that which alone would satisfy me. My heart delighted in the love Jesus offered me. I wanted to know in a deeper way the Person I had given my life to three years earlier. I must find out more fully what He was like and what He wanted of me. What a fantastic journey this was and with Someone who loved me and knew the way ahead.!

Other campus activities claimed more of my time. Participation in the 'Little Sister' programme, which provided a personal friend for newly arrived students from overseas gave me an opportunity to learn new customs and to try out new foods. I enjoyed times with this group and with my friend from India. Ushering for the Symphony Orchestra also provided me with many hours of enjoyable music. Life was crammed with activity.

That first, intense year was completed successfully and now three months were free. It would be great to spend this time in a useful way and so I decided to work at Manitoba Pioneer Camp in Canada. This was run by IVF for boys and girls, mainly from the Winnipeg area who came for two to four weeks during July and August.

I was thrilled to find the camp located in a remote area, only reached after a ten mile drive along a dirt road and a further two miles by boat to an island. It was in 'Lake of the Woods', on the border of the States and Canada and only a few miles, across the water, from where I had grown up. All around the camp were other islands also covered by pines which grew triumphantly on the bare rock. The rocks of the shorelines were gouged with deep scratches left by the glaciers as they scraped across the ancient Canadian Shield.

Here, like no other place, the summer evening sky displayed such lovely soft colours of sky blue, pink: a magnificent setting for the dark pines as they were reflected in the water. It was especially enchanting when the loons were out and their distinctive cry came to us across the water. The sound of these birds had a sad, haunting quality about them, that touched something deep within me and was the epitome of the North.

Canoeing through the early morning mists possessed a beauty all of its own. Some of us found it especially peaceful to get out early, to paddle gently across the still waters of the bay and enjoy the quiet before the busy day began. The lake was not always so calm and unruffled; sometimes violent storms churned the waters to a raging fury. Then I was quite happy to be on land!

Boys' camp saw me occupied as camp nurse tending to the inevitable variety of cuts and bruises and sometimes a slight case of home sickness. During the next month at girls' camp I was a counsellor, which meant I was responsible for a cabin of several young teenage girls. We enjoyed doing many things together such as canoe trips, cookouts and Bible Study. Life was busy and enjoyable; I could have stayed here forever.

The pines towering above me were whispering softly, I sat on the scarred rock trying to absorb the fleeting sight of sun playing with water. Light twinkled back at me from every wave; silver-shot blue washed at my feet: quiet peace.

Upon the water rode a golden leaf. There was still the warmth of summer yet it foreshadowed, in its colour, the coming autumn and my return to university. I hated to leave; it had been a rewarding and healing summer for me.

The hurt lay still and deep inside. Where are you my child? The oil of God's love soothed the sharp pain of grief.

'It's all right, I love you and your son. Just trust me.'*

When I got back to the university in the autumn I wanted to encourage others to go and work at Pioneer Camps and be a part of the great impact it had on campers' lives. So at one of our first IVF meetings of the year I got up and made an announcement.

'I'm looking for a man! . . . to serve next summer at Pioneer Camp.'

I went on to describe the work involved; announcing it this way would probably attract people's attention. Indeed it did! I was told later my announcement really caught one man's attention and he wondered who on earth this girl was.

It was a lovely crisp, sunny October Sunday as I walked into the International Students Bible study and saw several new faces. One person in particular caught my eye.

'Who could he be? He looks pleasant,' I mused. 'He looks different, a bit more mature, or perhaps it's just because his hair is slightly grey, a nice salt and pepper mix!'

At the end of the study, as we enjoyed our cups of coffee, introductions were made and I found Eric, for that was his name, to be very likeable. He had such a delightful English accent. There was a quiet thoughtfulness about him, different from anyone else I'd ever met. His eyes were gentle and he had a ready smile. I found myself liking him immediately and during our Bible study discussions it became obvious he was also a Christian.

In the weeks ahead the group members became better acquainted and Eric and I often talked together.

'How do you like Minnesota?'

'Oh, it's very different, especially at this time of year. I never expected such brilliant coloured leaves but it certainly was cold a few nights ago. It was much colder than I've ever known, and it's not even winter!'

'Well, it'll get a lot colder yet,' I replied, and others laughed knowingly.

'How long have you known the Lord, Eric?'

'Just over four years, and you?'

'That's interesting, I have too. It must have been about the same time but on opposite sides of the ocean.' We went on to fill in some of the details.

'One of the things that made me think was when an old man stood up in our Christian Union meeting at University College and described his years of "fellowship with the Risen Christ". I didn't know what he meant, but a few months later I found out and began that same relationship with Christ.'

'Well, in my life, the Lord had to lead me through some very difficult times until I saw my own need of Him,' I replied.

What a wonderful thing it was to be able to share with Eric, he was so easy to talk to.

It was not long before he was asked to join us on the executive as we led the group and his sense of humour endeared him to all.

Some months later, in the Spring of that year, the

phone rang as I sat at supper with friends, one of whom went to answer it.

'It's for you Nancy.'

'Who is it?'

'It's Eric,' she replied with a smile.

With surprise I went to the phone.

'Would you like to come out for dinner with me sometime next week?' he asked.

I was stunned but replied, 'Yes . . . that would be nice.' We had been just friends for some months, and I had not expected a date with him.

As I resumed my seat at the table five questioning faces were turned to me.

'What did he want?'

'Oh, he just invited me out for dinner,' I tried to be casual.

My friends smiled again!

Later that week we went out for a lovely meal and spent an enjoyable evening talking together. But that was that. He didn't ask me out for another date although we did go with a mutual friend to see my home town and met my parents.

The following November Eric returned to England after spending just over a year at the university. I felt unhappy and sad. I was going to miss a dear friend. All of us had grown to deeply admire him. Eric wrote casually a few times and I was glad to keep up the contact.

The rest of the year for me continued its frantic pace. I completed all my courses and my Public Health Nursing field study. It was enjoyable to be out of doors as I did my rounds of home and clinic visits and put into practice what I'd learned. This was the life for me.

There was the incentive of planning a trip to Europe in the Spring. I had dreamed of doing this for many years; it would be a trip in company with two girl friends. We would go after graduation in June. There was a real wanderlust in me, born out of years of reading books on travel.

'Ann, maybe we could get Eric to be our guide while

we are in London. It would be useful to have a "native" show us around.'

'Yes, why don't you write him and ask if he would mind doing that.'

So the letter was sent off and he accepted with pleasure.

4: Two Shall Be Born A Wide World Apart

Two shall be born a whole wide world apart,
and one day, out of darkness,
shall stand and read life's meaning in each others
eyes.
Anon

My university work was finished. I was itching to leave for my trip to Europe and see at last the places I'd only read about; dreams would become reality.

First I needed to go to Germany and pick up my Volkswagen at the factory. My two girl friends, Barb and Ann and I would travel around Europe in it and then ship it back for use in my new job. So began our trip which would take us from Italy to Scandinavia and all the places in between. Everything was completely new and different and we found it absolutely fascinating.

The youth hostels we stayed in were an interesting mixture; they ranged from medieval castles to tiny houses. One we particularly loved was in Switzerland. We were snuggled warmly under our puffy eiderdowns in small carved wooden beds set into the wall. We slowly drifted into consciousness to the sound of church bells. I walked to the window and looked out;

'Ann and Barb come see, the mountain has turned to gold!' The rising sun was touching the snow on the Matterhorn with a glittering finger.

'Oh, that's gorgeous! Let's hurry up and climb it.'

'Well I'm not going to the top but we should get a good hike in as we have all day.'

I stood there looking with fascination up the street from the hostel window. The buildings echoed the room's interior with their carved wooden designs and colourful flowers in windowboxes. People were already bustling about their daily routines and the tinkling of the cow bells came on the still, morning air.

I leaned on my elbows at the window watching the changing spectacle of the busy village life. This trip was just as I had imagined it would be. Fascination, excitement, interest; it was a dream being lived. Years of reading travel books had given me a hunger to see things for myself and I was drinking it in thirstily.

'Come on Nancy and get dressed; you can't stay there all day. We want to get going.'

There were other vignettes of that summer; people carrying home their bread, the long loaves strapped to the backs of their bikes; sitting in an Austrian mountain meadow surrounded by wild flowers; Michelangelo's Moses, in flowing marble robes; the dark horror of Belsen concentration camp; the quiet beauty of Amsterdam and its canals; the Swedish countryside looking just like Minnesota. Delicious pastries, snitzels, boullabaiasse, fondues. . . !

We spent ten glorious days in Norway with my friend, Else, who proudly showed us around her homeland. We had met the previous year at university, when she was doing post-graduate work. Now we could see her beloved country for ourselves.

What scenery! The fjords with the narrow roads bordering them; waterfalls around every corner; seeing Bergen in the twilight of the midnight sun; it all delighted us. We stayed at her mountain cabin and went for long walks and collected thick fresh cream from the nearby dairy.

We left her reluctantly but after almost 8000 miles on the continent it was time to ship my car back to the

United States to await my arrival a month later after our tour of England.

We drove to Hamburg to have the car shipped home and with one short flight we were in London at last. We immediately picked up our guide, Eric, and exhausted him as we tried to see every last tourist attraction. Only crazy Americans have to see everything, and all at once.

How good it was to see Eric again; it was such a pleasure just to be with him. We all enjoyed his delightful company.

Our few days in London were over and we bade farewell to Eric. We wanted to see more of the country. I wanted to go and yet didn't. I felt restless.

It was a grey, drizzly afternoon when we left. Once more I had a deep sense of sadness and wished I could stay and see more of him. I would miss my friend and didn't know when I'd see him again.

Barb returned home, and Ann and I were on our way to spend three weeks hitch-hiking around England, Scotland and Ireland. We tramped many miles around the small islands, met many friendly people and grew to love the countryside.

'This can't be August, I can't believe this weather. It's so cold! Ann, I feel mouldy.' I said as we stood by the roadside, shivering, waiting for a lift.

'Yes, me too,' she replied, 'we probably are with all this cold and constant rain. That last hostel, in the castle, near Inverness must be the coldest place on earth. How do people survive here in the winter? This is supposed to be summer!'

The last few days of our trip were not planned in detail, Ann was going to visit her pen-pal for four days and I had nothing special to do. Then I found out that my aunt and uncle were going to be in London and I decided to see them and visit Eric again if possible.

So I wrote to Eric. 'Can I have my guide back for the last few days? I'm going to be in London.'

Our letters crossed in the mail. 'Nancy, can I see you again before you fly home?'

So I returned to London and we visited my aunt and uncle and did more sightseeing. Eric took me to one of the famous Promenade concerts in the Royal Albert Hall, I was surprised at all those noisy, enthusiastic folks.

'Eric are they really British?'

'Of course,' he laughed, 'you don't really know the English . . . yet!'

Afterwards we went for a stroll in Hyde Park. It was a lovely evening, soft and warm.

'I love you! Will you marry me?'

Eric's words left me stunned. His completely unexpected proposal was the last thing I imagined I'd hear. Were my ears deceiving me? How could this be? My feelings were completely mixed up. I liked Eric so much, but I was afraid; afraid to care deeply again for anyone and yet I knew that he was different.

'Eric you're a wonderful man, a very dear friend but I don't know if I love you', I tried gently to explain this to him.

The tears came unprompted as I said, 'I'm afraid to care again. I'm afraid of a close relationship as I was once very deeply hurt when I dared to love someone. I like you so much but just don't know if what I feel towards you is love, yet.'

Eric didn't pry or comment on my words but just held me close as we talked; I longed to be more specific, tell him why I was so afraid to trust, and of the pain from the past. If only I could tell him the whole story I was sure he would understand. But his words had come so suddenly they caught me unawares and unprepared.

The next day passed by in a dream; we went to Kew Gardens, walked around St. James' Park and I became aware that I really WAS in love with this delightful man! I was sure now Eric was the one the Lord had chosen for me! I became aware, in the space of those few hours, of my love for Eric and began to see the reason for the sadness which had characterized our previous partings. The Lord had been drawing my heart, unknowingly, towards Eric for some time.

God had allowed me to know Eric thoroughly, just as a friend, so that I was able to see his qualities in a detached way. Now I sensed the Lord saying, 'Yes, this is the one I have chosen. You can trust yourself to him.'

We had two short days together before I flew home. There was so much to talk about and so much more that needed sharing but there wasn't the right opportunity to do so. I longed to tell Eric of the birth and relinquishment of my child but was hesitant to do so. Was this the right time? Should I say anything at all? After all, those events belonged to a closed chapter of my life. The Lord had forgiven and forgotten and I must as well.

I did want to tell him, but how could it be done and what should be said. The right moment never came in the next two days and then I had to leave. We had crammed so much into such a short time. What a difference those few days had made to my whole life!

Our parting at Euston was difficult. My reluctance to leave Eric must have been apparent to my fellow travellers, one of whom remarked, 'Never mind love, you'll see him again soon.'

It was meant kindly but the lady who spoke could not possibly have understood what was going through my mind as I thought of other partings; of the baby I had had to leave. Now to leave the man I loved with no idea when we would be together again was doubly hard.

I was sure in my heart, Eric was the right one but told him I must get back home and then give him my answer to his proposal. I needed a chance to think everything through; just to be sure that my decision was not taken on the spur of the moment and in a strange country.

I really knew what that answer would be! And knew he did too but since things had happened so fast I must wait to give a definite 'Yes' until I got home.

When I rejoined Ann later that day for our flight to New York she exclaimed, 'something happened. I think you're in love with Eric!'

'How do you know?'

s.c.—3

'Anyone can see from the glow on your face!'

It still didn't seem possible, I felt absolutely thrilled.

I drove alone from New York the 1500 miles home to Minnesota in just two days. I was in a hurry to tell my parents the good news and as soon as I saw them the news was just blurted out.

'I'm getting married – to Eric.'

They were pleased by my happiness and fortunately they had met him once so he was not a total stranger to them.

I telegrammed to Eric, 'Yes. Set the date!'

Eric's response was immediate. 'As soon as possible! Prov 19:14'.

Love had burst in upon me but how I missed him! It was hard to be apart and only be able to share by letter, which we began immediately to do.

'Dearest Eric, It's only a few days since we were together and I can hardly believe it all happened! How wonderful it is to have your love. I don't deserve it but know, like God's love, it's a gift and I joyfully accept it. I will try to love you as I ought.

Your love is deep and secure and a love I've never known before. It's so hard to have you so far away. . .'

It was not long before a blue envelope with a London postmark appeared in our mail box. I ripped it open quickly.

'Darling, life is so empty here with you gone, but we know this separation is really a time of preparation. It's hard, but He will prepare us through it for our life together. When two people in love are apart there will be pain but He will help us to bear it as we come to Him. All my love, Eric.'

A couple of weeks later I drove to Illinois to begin my new job. Once again life was busy and my mind kept occupied as I was thrust into a new situation beginning as a Public Health Nurse. I had accepted this position, just north of Chicago, before I left on my European trip and knew I owed it to my employer to work for at least a year. In any case, we weren't sure exactly when Eric could re-enter the States and we could be married.

My work was varied and interesting. It involved doing home care, follow-up on communicable diseases, health teaching in the schools, and covering numerous other aspects of Public Health. I was fortunate to have a helpful group of experienced nurses to work with and learn from.

My deep loneliness at having Eric so far away was eased by friends I made at church and work. It was important to enter into community activities and not mope around so I began visiting in the local psychiatric hospital, just to show friendship.

A night class in Spanish was also begun to help me communicate with some of my patients who were migrant workers from Mexico. It was an unequal task! Just as in my previous experience with a foreign language I had great difficulty memorizing and so had to drop it after a few months.

Our letters continued; we wrote almost every day. '. . . Eric do you realize only two months ago I didn't even know I was in love with you but now its deepening every day.

You know my doubts and questions but I want to be yours, it will be worth it even to leave my home and friends and my independence!

I have said before I'll need to learn to give myself and relate to others, yet so often I hold back to protect myself from being hurt. You will have to be patient with me.'

Many times I wondered about writing and telling Eric about my child and finally made an appointment with my pastor in order to ask his advice.

I was apprehensive about the meeting. Would he tell me to share the story with Eric and could I bear to do that? So I sat facing the Pastor, his desk between us, and the story was quickly told. No one else had heard me tell this and if he was surprised he didn't show it. When I had finished he spoke reassuring words.

'Nancy, it's in the past and it's forgiven. You must forget it and it serves no purpose at all to tell Eric.'

What relief those few minutes conversation brought. But what else could he have said? It put him in a difficult situation. His decision might have caused the end of our engagement and would that be right? Rightly or wrongly, I took his advice and said nothing to Eric and tried to live in the present and forget what was gone.

Memories. The hurt and grief ran like a silent river just under the surface of my awareness. I lived as normally as possible but there was the empty ache inside. Where was my boy? He was growing up, now six years old. I was sure he must be in a good home and progressing normally, but where?

I grieved for my child in secret; my practice over the years had enabled me to hide this, and to others nothing showed.

Eric and I kept the mailmen busy with our frequent letters during the following months. We tried to pour out our feelings and hopes for the future and get to know each other better.

'Nancy, I'm so lonesome but the Lord in His time will bring us together. I'm still amazed how we found each other; won't we have a wonderful story to tell our children some day!'

I wrote back, 'We certainly will! I can't stand this being apart. If only I can keep my eyes on Christ and endure, knowing the joy He has in store for us.

By the way, Eric, did I ever let you know my friends have often said I would never meet a man who could afford to feed me. Can you?

I'm having such fun telling people here how the Lord brought us together, I just want the whole world to know!'

Early in October I answered a knock at the door. There stood the mailman with a registered parcel for me. I hurriedly opened it and found to my great surprise a beautiful engagement ring and with it a note from Eric.

'I've chosen this ring especially; when you see its three

diamonds you will know it signifies – me, you and our love united by Christ in the centre.'

It was lovely! I was proud to wear it and counted the days until we would be together again.

During those long months apart Eric and I found ourselves in a situation where we must practice what we preached. We had to come to appreciate that Christ was the answer for every circumstance. Now we had continually to go to Him and let Him help us cope with our sadness at being apart, at our longing to see each other and be together.

We often quoted 2 John 12 to each other, 'I have much to write to you, but I don't care to put it down in black and white. But I hope to visit you and talk with you face to face, so that our joy may be complete!'

It was comforting to know we were praying for each other at the same time each day, Eric at 10pm in England and I at 4pm. We knew we had to depend on the Lord first of all, have Him fill our lives, or our love for each other could draw us away from a complete commitment to Him.

June came at last. It had been a long year with only three phone calls to ease the loneliness. Now we had three lovely weeks to be together when I flew to London for my summer holidays.

Our summer reunion at Heathrow was joyous after ten months apart. My Englishman looked better than I'd remembered. Joy! This was also the time to get to know my future mother and sister-in-law. But there were some initial difficulties with the language.

One day when we were at Eric's mother's and friends were in, a question about the rain produced the following exchange of words.

'Neh, as it gid oer?'

'It's not gi'd oer. It's bin agate aw neet.'

'Eric what are they saying?' I whispered. 'Is it a different language?'

'No,' he laughed, 'it's only Lancashire dialect. You'll soon be able to understand it too. I'll translate: "Now has it stopped?" "It hasn't stopped." "It's been at it all night." '

I was a source of amusement when I couldn't follow a lot of the conversation but everyone was very warm and friendly. It didn't matter, Eric and I were together.

The three weeks went all too quickly and we had to say goodbye again, but this parting was softened by the prospect of our wedding in a few months.

Once again I was back at work and back to our letter writing. '. . . the days drag by but October will soon be here and we will be together with no more goodbyes for a while. Eric, these words on marriage from an article, in His Magazine struck me as important.

' ". . . I am not simply to love my wife because I like am to love her so that in and through this marriage she may find new depths to her being in her response to others and to God. In the last analysis I am not to be pleased but she is to grow in the fullness of the nature God allowed her. I am to catch God's vision for her." '

Eric wrote back, 'with the Lord's help I hope to do that dearest.'

We began to make our wedding plans in earnest; long distance plans – I was 500 miles from home and Eric was 4500 miles in the other direction. In spite of this everything was planned without any real difficulty.

Of course the days and weeks did pass; summer finished, the leaves began their pageant of colour. I had to say goodbye to friends in Illinois, finish my job and go home for the last week before the wedding.

The last of our travel arrangements were sorted out and my Englishman arrived in Minnesota just three days before the wedding. Eric's mother and sister had come a few days before that, having sailed over.

What an eventful year this had been! So much had happened. My joy was full.

5: Whither Thou Goest

Be subject to one another out of reverence for Christ.

Wives be subject to your husbands, as to the Lord.
Husbands love your wives, as Christ also loved the
church and gave Himself up for it.
In the same way men also are bound to love their
wives as they love their own bodies.
A man shall leave his father and mother and shall be
joined to his wife and the two shall become one flesh.
Each of you must love his wife as his very self;
and the woman must see to it she pays her husband
all respect.

Ephesians 5:21–22, 25, 28, 30–31, 33

Where you go, I will go,
and where you stay, I will stay.
Your people shall be my people
and your God, my God

Ruth 1:16

An autumn wedding in Minnesota involves a risk with
the weather. Extremes of heat or cold are possible. The
humidity of the summer, with its plagues of mosquitoes
is definitely gone, but the possibility of snow and really
bad weather is there too. We knew we were taking a
chance in this respect when we planned our wedding for
the 19th October. The days prior to that were fine, the
forecast good and the long awaited day surpassed our
expectations.

The trees were still clothed in bright gold and flaming red and as the morning mist cleared the temperature climbed. By afternoon, the time of the wedding, the day was glorious with brilliant sunshine. We could not have asked for anything better.

I felt the same way inside as I prepared for the ceremony; thrilled and excited to think that at last we would be together. Sometimes it had seemed only a dream. But I WAS getting married, to the man I loved and knew Eric was the one I wanted to spend the rest of my days with. My heart danced with gratefulness for all the Lord had given me.

This was a day of celebration, for the love we had for one another, uniquely given by the Lord. It would be a celebration shared with family and friends who were gathered from far and near. We realized that many who could not be with us, scattered all over the world, were praying and thinking of us. We were aware too that Christ was present as He had been long ago at that wedding in Cana.

So many things raced through my mind as I dressed. Just a few years ago my life seemed utterly and completely ruined and it seemed I'd never know happiness again. I was filled with a tumbled mix of bittersweetness. There was still my wound of grief but it was being bathed now in joy, so the pain was dulled. God was good; He was giving me hope and a future with the one I loved.

I felt relaxed, enjoying every minute of this wonderful day. My footsteps were light as I walked down the aisle on my father's arm and there at the front of the church was Eric, smiling and waiting for me. We two stood side by side holding hands, and made our vows – 'for better or for worse, till death do us part'. We exchanged our rings which we had bought together last summer. They had been inscribed inside with, John 15:12. 'Love one another as I have loved you.'

One of the songs chosen for our service contained words from the book of Ruth. 'Whither thou goest I will go, thy people shall be my people.'* I was doing what Ruth had done, leaving all that was familiar for a new country with a new culture and new family. However much I would miss my own family, friends, and country this was what I had happily chosen.

After the reception we waved goodbye and headed north in my Volkswagen. Little had I thought, when I picked it up in Germany just over a year ago, that it would be used on my honeymoon. We chose to spend our first days together in northern Minnesota's, 'Canoe Country', a few miles from the Canadian border. This was the land we both loved, the land of countless lakes, rugged rocks and forests, of great peace and beauty and few people. It was ideal for a honeymoon!

Our small log cabin was set among the tall whispering pines beside a lake reflecting the fall colours of the trees. The sun continued to shine for us as we walked the trails, canoed and fished. It was incredibly delightful just to be together and we cherished every minute; we had been separated so long.

We returned to my parents to spend the last few days and complete the remainder of our packing with the help of friends. Most of the baggage had already gone to the ship on which we would soon sail.

On our last evening at home Eric and I went out and stood in the backyard by the river. In the dusk the reflections of the trees in the water mingled with the last of the sunset's colours. It was a view typical of Minnesota and I loved it but now viewing it I felt sad.

'Maybe I'll never get to see this again. We might not be able to afford the trip back to see my folks, and as they get older. . . ,' I faltered.

Eric held me close and tried to comfort me, 'we can never tell but we'll try to return sometime.'

'I know it's worth it dear, just to be with you. The Lord will make it up in other ways.'

I was sad but at peace as we turned and walked up the slope to the house to rejoin the others.

Our journey back to England was quite an introduction to life at sea; the North Atlantic in early November is notorious and we experienced some of the worst of its wild weather. I was not aware before that ships could move in three directions at once! Up and down, sideways, twisting. The decks were roped off for most of the trip because of the gale force winds and the wild spray which was constantly flung across the ship.

Even upon our arrival at Southampton the weather seemed no better; everything was bleak and grey. This was England! My new home.

The taxi pulled away and we stood there in front of the big house, surrounded by a mountain of baggage.

'Here we are Nan. Our home. It's lacked only you.'

'Our apartment is on the top floor I remember you telling me that.'

'It's called a "flat" dear.'

'Another of the words I have to relearn. Think I'll manage?'

'I'll help you,' he laughed, 'but we'll have to take the suitcases upstairs by hand as there is no lift.'

'No what? I'll never learn', but I did.

We had arrived in Harrow and I was eager to begin to make our simple place into a comfortable home for us. Here we would begin to put together the dreams and plans for our lives. And put up the curtains!

The weather was depressing; it was very different from the cold, crisp, sunny Minnesota winters. I wrote to my parents and asked if there still WAS a sun, as I had not seen it for so long. They reassured me it was still shining brightly.

I was amazed as Eric and I settled into our new life together that we encountered few problems adjusting to each other. This was surprising since I was VERY independent, strong-willed and used to going my own way for 25 years. Oh, we had our disagreements and times of misunderstanding but they didn't last for long. I wanted a good marriage and was determined to work at it and God gave a gentle but strong husband to help me. We were both determined to keep Christ central and He gave us deep joy and happiness in each other. Our friendship and love were strengthened.

People were very curious to meet the foreign wife Eric had brought back and I was warmly welcomed. They were surprised that I wasn't too strange and we enjoyed learning new customs from each other and laughing at each others' accents.

The warmth of everyone's welcome made up for the lack of sunshine. Whoever said the British were staid and unbending? It was great getting to know Eric's friends and becoming acquainted with a new style of worship. Our local parish church services showed me a real sense of reverence as well as good preaching. But I froze, for the churches were SO cold although they claimed to have heating!

Eric was busy with his job as a research chemist in a local company and I found part-time work nearby as a District Nurse. It was difficult and frustrating finding my way around Harrow and the vicinity on my bicycle. The streets didn't run straight like those I was used to, nor did they keep the same name for long and so I got lost innumerable times. Then after a rather nasty spill on the bike my concerned husband grounded me!

Fortunately the agency car was mine to use for a while; it was an old Anglia, with a unique and not very efficient heater – a hot water bottle. That car could also be very temperamental and on cold mornings it took at least three hands to run; one to steer, one to hold the choke out and one to reach over and knock down the sticking semaphore turn signals. It was unlike any other car I had driven! But it got me to the homes I needed to visit.

The language was not the same as so many other Americans have found to their amazement. After several blank looks I found it necessary to learn a whole new vocabulary to make myself understood by others, especially by my patients.

'Let's see if we have all your things ready for when I've finished giving your bath. Where is your underwear? Oh, I forgot, do you have your vest and knickers out?

And where is your washcloth, bother, I mean your face flannel.'

Will I ever learn the language? I ticked off in my mind some of the new words I had encountered; porridge, tea towel, cottonwool, jumpers, serviettes, and the list went on and on. Friends had lots of fun teaching this ignorant foreigner how to talk properly.

Shopping for food proved another challenge.

'Do you want a joint, love?'

'A what?'

Once I had got it how did I cook it? Roast it, fry it, boil it? My friends helped me and I appreciated the honesty of the storekeepers as I struggled, with difficulty, to work out how much change to expect for 13s-4d worth of groceries. Even if I knew how much to expect it was difficult to make sense of the handful of strange coins in my hand.

It was enjoyable shopping in the little shops with their lovely fresh food and then coming home with my purchases to fix meals for Eric. Amazingly, he adapted with ease to many foods which were new and different. Our life together was good and I often stopped to thank God.

One thing I found difficult however, was when I could not plan ahead; it made me feel trapped and hurt. Was this because of the need from the past to have something out ahead to hang on to; a future prospect to keep me going and if I didn't have that, was it too difficult to bear?

My inner pain lay there undisturbed except on rare occasions when I would wonder what had happened to my child. It cut deep as the remembrance of my tiny crying baby came to me. Once more I felt myself walking down the long, long hall alone and the bitter anguish of my loss was overwhelming. My baby was gone forever.

I tried to forget and not think about the past. Usually I was successful and thought it was gone but it was still there lying hidden but coming to mind when I least expected it.

Eric's gentle, loving ways helped immeasurably. He was a good husband but his slow and sometimes indecisive ways often made me inwardly very impatient. I realized, though, that he had much more to put up with living with me!

Long before the two of us met we both wanted someday to go overseas. We were aware of the possibilities with missionary societies but also felt drawn to 'non-professional' missionary service.

A letter came in the mail that March, Eric opened it eagerly and read it through.

'Nan, its hard to believe. We've been offered a job teaching in a high school in Kenya. It's the same place as my school friend Jim teaches at.'

'That sounds exciting, how did they find out about us?'

'I suppose Jim told them. Do you remember last year I wrote and told you I was praying about going into teaching?'

'Yes, of course.'

'Well, I had prayed that in two years I might know what to do next. Whether I should stay in research or go into teaching. It's almost two years to the DAY of that prayer!'

'It looks like the Lord is leading us to consider this and you have often spoken about wanting to go to East Africa.'

'I know,' he said, 'but with you not well yet I'm not sure what we should do.'

I was just home from hospital; recovering from major surgery having had a large cyst and my appendix removed. I had not been well for months and they had finally found out what was the matter but it seemed to take forever to feel right again after my operation.

We prayed about this for a couple of weeks and eventually wrote accepting their offer. Shortly, a letter came back.

'We are sorry to say we have offered the job to someone else as we hadn't heard from you sooner.'

Our disappointment was acute as we were by then convinced this was the place we should go. A few weeks later we heard again from the school.

'The person we appointed has withdrawn. Are you still interested?'

Were we! There was no delay in replying this time, and so less than a year after my arrival in England, the trunks were out and the packing begun again. Just before our departure we were sent on a training weekend with forty others to learn how to live abroad. It was at centrally-heated Farnham Castle. But what a waste, it was 80 degrees outside.

September 4th, 1964, found us at Heathrow Airport sitting in the BOAC terminal; it seemed like a dream. Were we really going to live in Kenya?

I was reminded that eight years ago to the day I was entering nursing and feeling I would never recover from my grief at losing my child. God had indeed healed much; the hurt was dulled but it was still there like a time bomb inside of me.

'Passengers for Nairobi board through Gate 4.'

'Nan, that means us!'

We gathered our things together and made our way with the others to the plane. We felt excited as we boarded. The lights of London receded, we were on our way – there was no turning back now!

Later that evening our plane touched down to refuel in Benghazi, Libya and we took the chance to get out and stand for the first time on African soil. Sand stretched out in all directions. Here and there we saw a few palm trees on this small oasis; their fronds barely moved in the heat. Inside the airport building the ceiling fans were slowly turning, keeping the hot night air moving. It all seemed unreal; just like a scene out of an old movie.

We were in Africa! What lay ahead of us here? How long would we stay?*

6: Kenya – New Adventures

The Great Rift Valley

The ground dropped away in front of our feet as we peered over the edge of the escarpment. Down and down it fell, over 2000 feet, and out and across for 40 miles. The distant rim of the valley was indiscernible, lost in a dusty haze.

What mighty upheaval had formed this vast scar, thousands of miles long, across the face of Africa? What power still fuelled its bubbling hot springs and the boiling lava of Ol Doinyo Lengai?

How slight the hand of man rested upon it. The narrow road snaked its curving path down the side and across its breadth, the tiny cars moving silently along. The sun glinted off the toy-like train far below beginning its labouring ascent of the steep incline.

Pools of silvery blue shone in the heavy light: Naivasha, Nakuru, Elementeita. Lakes still unexplored by us but with magic in their names; days of delight there still awaited us. Africa! Adventure unlimited!

We woke shortly after dawn and soon had our noses pressed against the window of the plane. Far below us was an immense river stretching out in all directions.
'This is the captain,' the voice over the loudspeaker

announced. 'We are now over the Sudan. The river you see now is the Nile. We'll be over Ethiopia shortly and in another hour over Northern Kenya.'

Soon the land we flew over became drier and very rugged. There were sharp valleys and flat plateaus but everything was barren.

'Eric how can anyone exist in such inhospitable looking country? It doesn't look like anything would even grow there.'

'Well they must somehow Nan, but it does look like a harsh land. I don't think Kenya is like this.'

The terrain gradually began to change; first just tinges of green and then extensive cultivated areas stretching out everywhere. This was the central part of Kenya; we would soon be landing in Nairobi. Our excitement grew.

As our plane descended we could see the land dotted with trees; then the buildings came into view; Nairobi looked bigger and more modern than we had expected. With a gentle bump we touched down, a new country, a new continent. We were eager to see with our own eyes what the books had already told us about this fascinating land.

Customs and immigration were cleared smoothly; we found everyone friendly and helpful. Jim, Eric's friend, was there to meet us.

'Welcome to Kenya, its great to see you. Come on I'll take you to Alliance; Judy and the others are eager to see you.'

We looked around like children. Everything was so different from any previous experience. Those first few hours and days were filled with wonder as we saw so much that was new. We saw smiling faces of every shade; palest brown to blackest ebony. How anaemic we Europeans looked by contrast. God gives man such an interesting variety of colours.

The grey, drizzly morning was quite unlike the sunny tropical one we had pictured.

'Is it always like this?' Eric asked.

'No, the sun does shine most of the time but we can have cloudy days too.'

Driving to the school we marvelled at the profusion of flowers of every shape and colour; along the centre median of the highway; cascading down the sides of buildings; and spilling out of gardens. The bougainvillaea especially caught our eye. Its vivid shades of pink, red and purple painted the houses and gardens with its glory.

The city was soon left behind and we started the climb to the village of Kikuyu, near where the school was located. It was 15 miles and 1500 feet higher. We passed circular thatched huts and saw young boys tending flocks of goats. The unusual dark, red-brown earth caught our eye as it formed many steep sided hills and valleys. This was all typical of this area – Kikuyu Country. It took us a good half hour to cover the distance up to the school; around yet another corner and there was Alliance High School.

It was famous all over East Africa but we didn't realize yet the full extent of its influence. The name was magic to hundreds of schoolboys who dreamed of being among the 'elect', the chosen few who gained entrance to the school after competitive examinations. From its doors had emerged men of authority and influence in government, business and the civil service, as well as those who were doing the unsung but vital day to day work all over the country.

It had been founded back in 1926 by a group of protestant missions and had for years been the only school in East Africa open to Africans wanting a secondary education. To Alliance came students from over 40 different tribes; here they learned to appreciate one another and work together. They were also challenged to reach the highest academic standards and to follow Christ.

Carey Francis, who had been its headmaster for over 20 years, had left a brilliant career as a Cambridge don to devote his life to the men and boys at this school. This tradition was now being carried on by another dynamic headmaster, Laurie Campbell.

He and his wife kindly invited us to stay with them for several days before we moved into our own house which seemed so huge for just the two of us. I had a deep longing for children to fill its rooms with laughter but was afraid, maybe I would never have another child. There was that ache as I thought of my growing son – somewhere, halfway around the world from me. It left such an empty void; an invisible wound of longing for what I had lost forever. Determinedly I pushed down these painful memories – today, I must live for today. The past cannot be changed.*

We stood on our large front verandah and looked at the view stretching out across the lawn with its flowers and poinsettia trees. We could see for many miles out across the plains to a range of hills in the far distance. From there came the wind, the unceasing wind. Eric held me close, it was a bit chilly.

'Well Nan, this is the tropics!'

'I didn't think it would be this cold.'

Closer by we could see steep, grass covered hills with cows grazing on them. This was where our milk came from, fresh, unpasteurized and delivered to our doorstep each morning. We walked up the road past our house and were shown the spot from which, on a clear day, we could see snow capped Mt. Kenya one hundred miles to the north.

I soon realized why the other staff had local people to work for them in their homes. I too needed someone to help me with the daily cleaning and polishing of acres of cement floors and the washing of all our clothes by hand, in the bathtub. We also had to boil all the water and milk we drank; it all took lots of time and energy.

Lucas, a Luo from western Kenya, came to us shortly after we arrived and stayed with us for our seven years there. He became very close to us as a family and an invaluable help. James, a local Kikuyu man, looked after the garden and he was kept busy especially during the rainy season for then the cutting of the grass was unending. He also chopped the firewood, since we needed a fire every evening. Eric was so busy with school he had no time to do these tasks.

We quickly became absorbed into the busy life of the school with its mixed but closeknit community of 20 European and African staff and nearly 300 boys. Eric began the brand new task of learning to teach and found Alliance a wonderful place to begin as the boys were eager and keen to learn. In the beginning it was tiring and difficult but he knew with certainty it was what he wanted to do.

He was also involved in many other activities since this was a boarding school with its games, societies and the supervision of dormitory life. My time was occupied with our house, garden and working part-time. This gave me little time to think of the past. I began volunteer nursing at the local Presbyterian Mission Hospital just a mile away.

The rusty-brown dust on the road sifted into my sandals as I climbed the steep hill to the hospital. Nothing was on the level around here, it was a constant up and down wherever one went. I passed several of the local Kikuyu women bent low under their burdens of wood or large drums of water.

I felt hot and tired; how must they have felt weighted down under their immense loads every day? They were such tiny women but strong and proud to be able to carry so much.

'Wimwega.' I said.

'Aaa nikwega,muno,' they replied.

I had learned to greet them in Kikuyu thus and received their polite response.

'How are you?'

'All is well.'

This was a new experience, to be teaching student nurses as well as helping to supervise in the operating theatre. My own experience in surgery had been long ago and in rather different circumstances. I was amazed at what the dedicated doctor and nurses did under very adverse conditions. In later years, with the help of overseas aid, a lovely new operating theatre and wards were built.

As wives, we were involved in most school activities. Some taught, some made costumes for the yearly Shakespeare play, and we all provided food for the school teas. We also began a girls' vocational training course nearby. I loved it all and was glad to be kept occupied so there was no time to brood about the past. But the thoughts would often come to me when I least expected it.

'How could you have given up your child, your own flesh and blood? You never loved him if you did that?' said an inner, tormenting voice.

How discouraged these thoughts would make me feel. Over and over and round and round, deeper in condemnation and despondency I'd drop. Then would come the realisation; those thoughts aren't from God!

How cunning satan is, how subtle in discouraging us. The Scriptures had taught me I needed to control what I thought about, 'we take every thought captive and make it obey Christ'.* Our wandering minds need to be brought back to focus on truth. I had to reject the fears and condemnation and state afresh, 'God loves me.' 'There is now no condemnation in Christ Jesus.' The Lord had taken my failure and had forgiven me. I knew He loved my son more than I could and would watch over him.

The hurt and grief over the loss of my child were buried deeper. I knew that many others carried scars of various kinds and I tried to focus on God and not the hurt. The happiness Eric and I shared together was healing.

Moreover I had never dared to expect that I'd be in Africa married to such a gentle, loving husband. Indeed, the Lord was good and had given me the desires of my heart, even though I hadn't specifically asked for them. I was largely unaware of how He had been guiding, providing and protecting me over the years.

We were glad to become better acquainted with some of the students when we had a group of them to our home for a weekly Bible study. Through this we became aware of their backgrounds and saw some of the great sacrifices their families had made to send them to school. Most of them had a very meagre income and struggled to get the fees although there was scholarship aid through the school. A family placed high expectations on a son privileged enough to have a good education, including providing money for schooling for younger brothers and the needs of all his extended family.

During our years in Kenya I tried to learn Swahili and encountered the same difficulty that I had experienced with languages before. English, with Swahili, was the official language in the country. Most of the students knew both as well as their own tribal tongue but all the teaching was done in English. I only managed to learn a dozen or so words of Swahili but this was enough and enabled me to do my shopping.

Much of my shopping could be done right at my back door when the local 'vegetable men' came round with their kikapu's (baskets) of fresh produce and a chicken, alive of course. A lot of my meat was bought in the local village of Kikuyu at one of the local 'dukas' (shops). The price was the same whatever the cut of meat; therefore we enjoyed filet mignon often.

Once a week we went into Nairobi to do major shopping; there one could purchase almost anything. In the local fruit and vegetable market bargaining was the 'name of the game' and I soon became quite expert at it. What an array of colourful Kenyan produce to choose from; juicy pineapples, oranges, bananas, avocados. We later developed a taste for more exotic fruit; mangoes, passion fruit, paw paw.

'The memsahib like this mango? Very good.'

'How much?'

'Shilingi tatu. (three shillings) It's very sweet.'

'That's too much; its kidogo(small),' I said.

S.C.—4

61

So might typical bargaining proceed, everyone enjoying it!

Like thousands before us, we fell in love with Kenya and its people. The country was endowed with a rich array of natural wonders, beautiful countryside and wild animals. We saw a lot even on short day trips. We also took longer safaris around the country in the months and years ahead.

We enjoyed just sitting in our garden and seeing the beautiful birds all around us; the large high flying kites with their mewing cry and the little sunbirds like sparking jewels. These flitted from flower to flower and reminded me of hummingbirds in Minnesota. At breakfast we were often serenaded by the grey and yellow bulbuls perched on our verandah. Their liquid notes were a wonderful start to any day.

A short drive could take us into Nairobi game park where we would stop the car and watch the herds of wildebeast, zebra and Thompson's gazelles feeding. It was though they were on a huge stage; there in the vast panorama of the dry dusty plains dotted with acacia and fever trees. This was backdropped by the purple haze of the Ngong Hills. A few minutes more and it was a different scene as we drove down the banks of the Athi River and watched crocodiles sunning themselves.

We felt so fortunate living and working here while many people travelled thousands of miles and at great expense to see this land. It was ours to enjoy in just a short hour's drive.

Often we would see animals while just driving along the highway or even in our own yard. Dik-dik tiny deer, only sixteen inches tall, wandered through our garden and ate our roses. They apparently found them very tasty! During the dry season monkeys might come swinging through the trees.

We were warned shortly after our arrival about a frightening night-time noise which came from the tiny innocent looking tree hyrax. They were hardly ever seen but after dark one could hear the sudden sound of a creaking door followed by a blood-curdling scream. This was well described as the despairing shriek of someone being strangled!

I expected to find lots of mosquitoes or snakes in Africa but saw few in all our years there, mainly because of our high altitude. We only saw them occasionally when on holiday at the coast. But there were countless flying ants and fat sausage flies both of which our cats loved to chase and eat. Termites were a nuisance, getting in the house as well as killing trees in the garden. Their six foot high homes of rusty coloured earth could be seen all over the country.

I loved to watch the rains come; the large rolling mass of dark clouds moving ever closer. The trees stood etched against its darkness and the hush fell as everything waited for the storm to break.

When the dark grey curtain of rain was just beyond the nearby hills it wasn't long before we would have to take cover. When the deluge hit us, it became impossible to hear much as it beat upon our tin roof. It also turned the unpaved roads to deep seas of mud. The rains were always welcomed by the small farmers as it was the life blood for the crops on their 'shambas'.

Most of the year we enjoyed warm sunshine in the day and cool evenings when we appreciated the warmth from our fireplace. During the rainy season my usual attire was not a sundress but wool slacks and sweater and then we kept the fire going all day long. This seemed strange since we were only 90 miles from the equator but the altitude was almost 7000 feet. If it were not actually raining, a clammy mist might hang around all day and this explained why pneumonia and bronchitis and not tropical diseases were so common. And why so many Scots settled in this area!

Holidays, often spent at the coast, on the shores of the Indian Ocean, were a different matter. We would rent a cottage or stay with friends and spend hours in the warm water or wandering along the miles of beautiful white sand beaches and it seemed crowded when there were even a dozen others around. The 300 mile trip to Mombasa was a challenge in our early years when more than half of the way was still a dirt road but by the time we left, it was almost all paved.

It was 1966, we had completed an eventful two years. Eric and I had learned better how to live together in harmony. There were the ordinary days full of enjoyment. There were also days of irritation and impatience but they were quite rare. It was an ongoing adaptation and adjustment when two VERY different personalities were brought together. Our shared interest in books, music and outdoor activities brought us lots of enjoyment. Now we were going back to England to see family and friends on our first leave. I felt satisfied but tired and knew it would be good to have a rest.

We met friends there, an Anglican vicar and his wife, and saw an amazing change in their lives. They said it was because they learned how to allow the Holy Spirit to fill them. This was something new to us. We hadn't known anyone personally who had experienced this but our friends, quite ordinary people, clearly had a new found joy and ease in ministry. Talking with them put a new desire in my life. I wanted to know the Lord in the living and dynamic way they did but I felt so dry spiritually.

'Lord, I want to see your face. I want to know you in a deeper way', was the cry of my heart.

For some time in our staff Bible Study at Alliance, there had been a friendly disagreement between myself and one of the other teachers. He said we must just 'grit our teeth and plug on' in our walk with Christ and I objected to this even though I did not see anything other than that in my own life.

'Surely,' I would say, 'the Bible shows us a different picture of the way things should be. The early Christians were different. They had a power and love I don't have.'

I felt a great longing to know God more intimately and change my dry and ordinary walk with Him. There must be a better way than I was experiencing at present.

I believe God takes us at our word. He knows the deep desire of our heart and then sees to it that we are stimulated in our search for Him, if we really mean it.

As soon as we were back in Kenya from our leave, one of my friends lent me some books she had found interesting. I wept as I read them, for I sensed the touch of the Lord in the experiences described in these books. How they fed my hungry searching heart. Here were ordinary people who had seen the realities of God at work in their own lives. I found this confirmed in the Bible and I wanted all that Christ had to offer me. I was hungry and thirsty for more.*

Over the next few years I searched in earnest. A lot intervened as our family grew and difficulties came and life went on. And as He promises to those who diligently search, 'you shall find me'. I did; but not just yet.

7: Two Gifts

Sons are a gift from the Lord
and children a reward from Him.
Psalm 127:3

'You are pregnant.' The doctor sat down across from me and said those words which reached back over almost nine years but this time unspeakable delight accompanied them.

We had been living in Kenya for a couple of months when I became aware there was new life within me. Before we were married Eric and I talked about our desire for a family; we looked forward to having children so were overjoyed to find our hopes being fulfilled.

The small school community in which we lived was made up of many young families and we were only one of several couples who were expecting at that time. Eric had no idea of that intense longing I had for a child. Now I had a stable home with a loving husband, a caring environment in which to raise a child in love and security.

But a flood of memories came tumbling into consciousness with the news I was expecting! There was a mingling of sadness and joy as that secret sorrow surfaced again. Then grief over the child I did not have, was intermingled with the great happiness at the prospect of a child of our own. I was not the same person now. Searing grief and healing joy had moulded me.

I longed to tell Eric about the past but if I told him now I thought it would be a terrible blow and would hurt him deeply. I could not bring myself to do that, so the Lord would have to continue to help me bear it alone.

Eric was the typical expectant father and showed great concern for my well being. We were both so happy that there was a little one on the way; yet I hid my fear. Was this child developing properly and would everything go easily with the birth? A threatened miscarriage only fuelled this fear but soon everything settled down and it looked as though there would be no more problems. This time I would receive proper medical care throughout the pregnancy.

My normal voracious appetite was disturbed by bouts of nausea but the end of these, after nearly three months, coincided with a short holiday at the famous Outspan Hotel in Nyeri. This was our first real 'safari' to see some of the country and we enjoyed the hotel's famous food and I did full justice to the wonderful six course meals!

Eric went to the window and looked out. 'Well Nan, there's something unusual, snow on the equator.'

I came over and stood beside him and saw Mount Kenya with the setting sun's rays catching the snow and making it shimmer.

'It's lovely but hard to believe it's so warm down here and cold enough for snow up there.'

'I wonder if the others from school have reached the summit yet.' Many of the staff and students climbed the mountain.

'Maybe we'll do it too someday, but I don't feel up to it just now!'

The early days sped by with the care of the house and my work at the local mission hospital. I grew steadily and noticeably larger and our altitude of 7000 feet, combined with the ever present hilly terrain, kept me puffing.

My mind was preoccupied driving into Nairobi on one of my early visits to the doctor; I knew she must be told of my previous pregnancy. As a nurse I new there could be problems with a second child as I was Rh negative.

I didn't really want to say anything as Eric didn't know, therefore others shouldn't; but medically it was imperative, the doctor must know.

I noticed how lovely it all looked as I drove along; the first of the rains had refreshed everything. The jacaranda trees were wreathed in a purple haze of blossom; all around glistened clean and fresh, the birds madly singing. But I felt heavy. If only Eric could have been told about my child during those hurried days back in London after his proposal. Then I would not have to bear this alone. But it hadn't been possible and so my loneliness was inevitable.

I sat in the doctor's office and told the story again to only the second person to hear it. She understood why Eric had not been told and reassured me by saying that my secret would be respected.

The doctor assured me that the baby was growing right on schedule and she would keep watch on me. How different this pregnancy was from the earlier one! Now there was joy instead of sadness; hope instead of despair and I was surrounded by friends full of loving, encouraging concern and I could openly and proudly let my pregnancy be known.

Eric was equally delighted at the approaching birth of our child; but for me, there was always that thread of grief because a part of me was missing – my other child. I tried not to think of this but only delight in what I HAD. I could not live in the past, I told myself, and the past could not be changed.

Less than a year after we came to Kenya our son Andrew was born, but not exactly as expected. At the last minute he had to be delivered by caesarean section.

As I came out of the anaesthesia I asked to see my baby. 'Can I see him, is he all right?'

'No, not now you can see him later.'

My heart contracted in terror. Something must be wrong or they would bring him to me. In my nursing we had always let mothers see their babies right away – unless something was wrong with the child.

Finally after several hours of fighting my way in and out of consciousness and begging to see him they finally brought my son to me. At last I could see for myself and be reassured; he was a beautiful baby and looked perfect in every way. Now I could sleep in peace.

Eric came to visit the next day full of excitement. 'It's great to see you awake. Are you feeling OK now?' he leaned down looking concerned and gave me a kiss and a lovely bouquet of flowers.

'It was awful to see you yesterday when you were still unconscious. You looked so white just like in the hospital in Harrow. I hate to see you like that.'

'I'm alright dear, but I can't laugh or the stitches hurt, so no jokes for a while.'

'Did you see Andrew? Isn't he wonderful?'

'Yes, they brought him after I begged for a long time. I don't know why they didn't let me see him right away. I was awful groggy though and can't really remember what he looked like.'

'He looks perfect! But he was protesting loudly when I first saw him yesterday. I think he looks a bit like me, a high forehead.'

'Hope he has your brains too dear,' I said.

'I'm not sure you really want him taking after me.'

'They won't let me have him to feed until tomorrow. Because he was a caesarean he has to be "cot nursed" and I can't hold him until then. I miss him!'

'Well that's not long to wait Nan.'

But he didn't know it was an eternity for me because I didn't have that contact with my other baby.

Real contentment only came, when after two long days, I could actually hold my son close and study his tiny hands, ears, nose and look into his eyes. How precious he was to me!

As I held Andrew in my arms and looked at him I wondered what my other son looked like. Did he look anything like this when he was a baby? If only I could have really seen him. But I could not think about the past, just shut my heart and forget. Life had to go on now. The joy of holding Andrew poured over the pain, as a soothing ointment.

'You would have enjoyed being at school for the announcement of Andrew's arrival.'

'Why? What happened?'

'I got back just as the boys were going into the dining hall for supper and Laurie made the announcement. The place just erupted with cheers; I thought they would never stop.'

'Well of course a son does mean a lot: this is Kenya you know!'

Andrew was a delightful baby, bright, bouncy and alert; interested in everything around him from his very first days. No little detail escaped his interest. Our son captured our hearts and brought us untold joy, especially as I thought I would never have a child to care for and enjoy watching grow and develop. Here was a child to whom I could give my love unreservedly. Andrew learned to smile very early and never seemed to stop. What a delight! He was always so full of fun. We were quite sure no one enjoyed their child more than we did.

My mind often went back to another child branded on my heart and not forgotten.*

'Lord, where is he?'

I longed to know but could not, my other son was lost to me. He was gone forever.

Our joy soon became tempered by concern when Andrew became very ill at seven months, with gastroenteritis and had to be hospitalized. It was a heartbreak to take him to hospital and then go and leave him there alone. There was no 'rooming in' in those days; mothers were not allowed to stay with their children.

I had to leave my little helpless child, to turn and go out of that hospital room and leave him there all alone. It tore me apart. I wept as it awoke in me those buried hurts and memories of leaving another child.

Every day found me there with him for as long as possible and a week later we finally had him back with us and we felt complete again as a family. It was as though a big hole had been ripped out of our lives when our son was not there at home with us.

The months went by and we saw Andrew become sick frequently and not gain weight as he should. The doctor felt that he would improve if he had his tonsils removed and once more he was admitted to hospital when he was only two and a half. My heart ached as I had to leave my son once more alone in a strange hospital room. A terrible emptiness filled me.

'Its all right Nan, he's in good hands and will soon be home.'

'Yes but it's so hard to leave him.' And I could say no more as to why it was so difficult.

Andrew looked so forlorn and sad sitting there in the bed all alone. He was in for ten days and I spent as much time as I was allowed with him but it was never enough. What rejoicing on the day we were able to bring him home; now, we thought, he will at last be healthy.

A few months before this, when Andrew turned two, we welcomed his sister Jean into our hearts and home. Again Eric and I were thrilled by the pregnancy; it was wonderful to have our family increased. We had hoped for a girl this time and so were absolutely delighted by our dainty daughter. My heart's desire was satisfied.

Just before Jean was born I felt concerned about my ability to love this new baby as much as Andrew. Of course my fears proved absolutely groundless! Jean immediately and completely won her special place in our hearts. We didn't love her brother any the less but the Lord enlarged our hearts to love more. It's always amazing when it happens but love does that. We are given a special love for each one that is brought into our lives and our daughter certainly proved easy to love.

I stood there watching her sleeping peacefully in her basket and felt such wonder. She was so lovely; her tiny fingers curled around mine as I stroked them. My daughter! I was so blessed, God had given me so much.

It was delightful to see the attention and love which Andrew expressed towards his sister. Right from the beginning he seemed to enjoy her and we never saw any jealousy, only care and consideration. Jean's big brother obviously loved her and he liked to hold her.

As the months passed they spent many happy hours playing together. They would go on rides around the house, Jean in her baby walker, holding on to the back of Andrew's trike as he pulled her along. The sounds of their laughter filled our home just as I dreamed it would.

The large house and garden gave them lots of space to play. They also had the neighbour's yard or the whole of the school grounds with the big sports fields to use with their friends. It was an ideal place in which to raise our children. The students loved them and liked to play with them whenever they were around. The Africans love their own children and anyone elses.

Our two stood out because of their blond hair and often were the centre of attention. Whenever we went into Nairobi their smiles would charm the fruit stall holders and they'd be given an apple or banana.

One afternoon, as usual, we had gone to watch a school soccer match. Andrew and Jean went off immediately to join the other staff children. Andrew, at five, was a happy fellow, slightly built but a quick runner. Jean, two years younger, followed eagerly; her long blond hair flowing behind as she ran, trying to keep up with her big brother.

The group of children began to play together; sometimes watching the game, climbing trees or investigating the herd of goats belonging to one of the local boys.

The late afternoon sun shone down on us. It was hot now but soon it would be chilly, when the sun went behind the hill. Then the sweaters we brought would feel good. We sat watching the game and chatting with the other staff.

'Eric, aren't you glad we had our children out here? They have so many good things to do and lots of friends to enjoy. I'm so grateful.'

'Yes, they certainly are never at a loss for things to see or do. There is lots of space to burn off their energy.'

It was not many months until Andrew was sick again. Every six weeks one infection after another made him very ill; he would develop a chest infection which then produced asthmatic bronchitis. This caused many hurried visits to the doctor or into the hospital emergency room for medication so he could breathe once more. Several times he had to be admitted into hospital when he was especially bad. In spite of this, between illnesses he was on the go constantly, always bright and cheerful.

Whenever Andrew became sick there was my own private battle of relinquishment; each time I needed to learn to let go of him and place him in the hands of Jesus, into His care and protection.

'He's yours Lord, you gave him to us, now take care of him and please heal him.'

Each time I wanted to hang on and would fight letting go and so could not relinquish him easily; each time it was a whole new battle to trust God. I had lost one child, I feared to lose another. Could I trust Andrew into His care? Of course, deep down knew I could, but still each time I had to go through it all over again.

Andrew was the Lord's gift to us and I knew He loved him more than we ever could and yet it was hard for me to trust. There seemed to be almost a permanent knot of fear which slowly unwound, only to knot up again a few weeks later. I lived for years holding my breath and waiting for yet another bout of sickness. I wondered; would this one be too bad to respond to treatment? Would we get him to the doctor quickly enough?

Those years were times of battle and of terrible discouragement. They were also times of learning to trust and then failing, but knowing that the Lord was keeping hold of me. Thankfully I knew God loved me even when trusting was difficult. I wanted to and the Lord looks at the intent of our heart. There certainly wasn't any opportunity over those years to become complacent. I would walk through the dark valleys and climb out only to be plunged into yet another one.

Great times of fun were interspersed between the days

of worry over Andrew's health. He and Jean were such a delight to us. I was content, thankful for what I DID have and tried not to think about what was missing.*

Those were tiring days as they were both on the go the whole day; Andrew especially must have felt he would miss out on something if he slept, so he didn't. At least he slept very little and a lot less than his parents required!

Jean's arrival persuaded us at last, that some children required a normal amount of sleep and they could sit still long enough to be cuddled. How nice to have a cuddler after a wriggler! She loved to be held and would snuggle close to me; what a blessing this child was. Often they would both climb up on my lap and we would read a book together.

'Eric, remember you wrote and told me before we were married, "the best thing a father can do for his children is to love their mother"? I just wanted to tell you, you are being a good father, dear!'

We had such joy as we watched these two grow. I remained amazed that they were mine, such lovely children. Jean was tiny and dainty, quite unlike myself as a child. They didn't resemble me at all; as they both looked so much like Eric. It made me wonder what my other child looked like. Did he look like me at all?

Once more I'd close my mind to the agony I felt and go on with the daily tasks and deliberately wall off my grief. Sometimes the walls would crumble and the stab of pain would pierce deep. Put up the barriers, don't think about it, it's not there. Fool I was to think that was so.

The children have pleasant memories of Kenya; of happy days playing with friends in the garden, climbing all available trees, building tree houses, swimming, fishing and countless other childhood activities. They especially liked our trips into the Nairobi Game Park and the Animal Orphanage adjacent to it. This contained lost or orphaned animals. On one such visit the cheetah paced Jean as she ran alongside the outside of its cage.

That was great fun! Names of all the animals came easily as they saw them frequently in the game parks; their sharp eyes often spotted them long before we did.

We had some delightful holidays along the coast swimming in the warm ocean waters. The hours sped by as they searched along the white sand beaches for tiny shells and chased crabs.

Our life during this period was busy but satisfying. We had no thoughts that anything unusual was about to happen that day in April on the commonplace weekly drive into Nairobi. Exceptionally heavy rain overnight had washed out part of the shorter road into town so we had to take the longer route. When we were halfway to town the peaceful trip was dramatically interrupted.

Events happened so fast there was no time to avoid hitting the land rover as it turned across our path. Its construction and our speed made the collision equivalent to hitting a tank broadside. The land rover was tipped over and our car a write-off.

Andrew and Jean were securely strapped in at the back, as we were in the front and I was the only one with any injuries. My neck and back were hurt and extremely painful; this was the third whiplash for me in the space of ten years and this time the damage was extensive. In spite of weeks and months of physiotherapy and medication the pain didn't stop. For the next two years pain became my constant companion until the Lord intervened. It was a discouraging time and I often grumbled. Why did it have to happen to me, why did I have so much pain?

We enjoyed our years in Kenya immeasureably and were enriched by the experience of having lived there. What a heritage we gained from the people there as we learned from them about real hospitality and generosity. This was evident to us especially when we went for visits to the homes of our students. These people were often living a marginal existence as the land was poor in many areas and the rain not sufficient for their crops. In spite of this they, who had so little in a material sense, would give generously to us when we came as their guests. It was often a real sacrifice yet they treated us kindly and fed us well while in their homes. We were sent on our way with gifts of pineapples, chickens, or eggs. They were delighted to be able to do this.

Eric also noted this same generous attitude in those students under his charge who went out weekly to teach Sunday School classes at the local primary schools. This often meant walking many miles each way which they did cheerfully. We had a lot to learn from them about how to serve others. There was no prestige attached to that work; it was purely voluntary but it put into practice the school motto, 'Strong to Serve'.

The cost of following Christ was also lived out before us when in 1968 the problem of taking oaths came up once again among the Kikuyu. It meant death or severe beatings for Christians who would not participate in it; still they rejoiced that they were worthy to bear this for their Lord. The cost of their love for Him was high and a challenge to our own faith.

During our third, two year, tour of service we found ourselves faced with the decision about our future. Should we stay in Kenya indefinitely or was it time to return to England? It was not an easy choice for we had grown to love the people and the country and really felt it was our home. But increasingly we knew that we should go back to England; partly because of Eric's need to establish himself as a teacher in a system where he could work long term and partly for the sake of schooling for our children. Thus we came to the end of a very significant period in our lives, difficult in some ways but which held for us such fond memories.

With the ease of hindsight, it is clear that God used this time to generate in me a deeper hunger to know more of Himself. He wanted to prepare us for new experiences through which we would be able to receive more of the blessings He intended for us.

Those last few weeks were busy ones as we rushed to complete the necessary arrangements for leaving and moving to a new job in England. Early on a grey, drizzly, typical Kikuyu morning we drove out of the entrance of Alliance for the last time. We headed for the airport with very mixed feelings; it was hard to leave behind the many friends we had grown to love and yet we knew it was right to go.

8: So Much More

'. . . some lives are marked by a growing hunger
after God Himself. They are eager for spiritual
realities and will not be put off with words, nor will
they be content with correct interpretations of truth.
They are athirst for God and they will not be satisfied
till they have drunk deep at the Fountain of Living
Water.'
A. W. Tozer, The Pursuit of God

I'm thirsty Lord, fill me.

Oh, why had we ever come back? Row upon row of
houses, millions of cars and crowds of people everywhere
were so overpowering and made me feel hemmed in. I
longed for the sun and wide open spaces we had grown
to love in Kenya.

Someone remarked to me, 'Aren't you glad to be back
in "civilization" again?'

'I'm not sure, now I have to teach my children to fear,
to be cautious of people and in Kenya we had no concern
for their safety. There, children are highly valued.'

This move unsettled me; I missed our friends but it
seemed a deeper feeling of need. Was it the longing for
the child I'd lost? Would I ever get over his loss? Some
days I could forget but then the anguish would engulf
me once again. I knew enough to turn to the Lord and
each time Jesus would hold me close and ease the pain
and I could smile and laugh again. Life went on.

In a couple of weeks we were able to locate a suitable
house in Bristol, and after just a few more weeks we

were able to move in. A lot of paint and elbow grease transformed our roomy semi into a bright and comfortable home. The main drawback for Andrew and Jean was to get used to the small garden which seemed confining after the acres of space they had in Kenya. But they did like helping to get our garden planted that spring. They also had a fascinating time watching the family of baby blue tits in their nest in our apple tree.

It was good to be within visiting distance of Eric's mother and sister. While abroad we were able to see them only every two years. Family ties were important to us and we took every opportunity to get together. We were now close enough so their grandmother could spoil the children, enjoy them, and watch them grow up.

I had forgotten how lovely the English spring could be as we had not experienced one for seven years. Flowers were everywhere. Their lovely fragrance hung in the soft warm air. The world once again was fresh and green.

'Oh, to be in England now that April's there,' are familiar lines and now I experienced the same beauty of which the poet spoke.

April in Minnesota was usually very different, flowers might have to push through a foot of snow!

We soon became involved in numerous activities at our local Anglican church. There was a gap left by the close community we left behind at Alliance but we found an echo of this in the smaller house church meetings and a weekly Bible study with friends.

Molly and Harry Raiss, more than anyone else, were used by the Lord to make us feel at home in England. They, like several others at church, had experienced the Lord's touch of renewal in their own lives and we shared precious times of fellowship as we met regularly together.

When God gave me the desire for more of Himself He also brought me into contact with the right people. By now I knew that I wanted the Holy Spirit to be released fully into my life; yet I put off doing anything about it.

Our friends were kind but persistent as they saw the

pain I had from my back. Since the car accident the pain never left. I went once again to the doctor and for physiotherapy but nothing helped at all.

'Nancy let's ask God to heal your back?'

'Maybe later Molly, its not serious. I guess I have to learn to put up with the discomfort. I shouldn't bother God with such a minor thing.'

How often do we believe that lie? Didn't I know deep down that He loved me and cared about all the details of my life? Then why did I procrastinate about asking for His healing?

The subject of divine healing came up in our Bible Study soon after, one cold Sunday evening in February. While we were discussing this another friend from the church walked in. Martin had a ministry of healing given him by the Lord.

Molly turned to me and said, 'Now is a good time to pray for your healing Nancy. May we lay hands on you?'

Further delay and excuses were useless. 'Yes I want to be free of the pain.' I was tired of the burden of it.

Our friends gathered round and prayed, quietly and confidently asking Jesus to touch my back and completely heal it. Suddenly I knew that I would be healed; the Lord gave me the gift of faith at that point.

Several times during that night I woke and expected the pain to have gone. I felt a bit impatient; it was still there.

Morning came and when I opened my eyes I realized the pain was completely gone! Jesus had healed me!* In two days even the aching had left too. Here was thrilling evidence of God's specific love for me. How lovingly He had answered the longing of my heart for the reality of His presence.

Now that I was free from the bondage of pain I got busy immediately making a big rock garden and moving wheelbarrow loads of earth and stones without any discomfort. It was a delight to be able to tell others what a wonderful thing the Lord had done, yet I met some who denied it was the Lord's doing.

'It would have been better anyway.' They said. But it hadn't with the best of medical attention.

It was sad to see their denial but it couldn't take away the fact nor the joy of my healing. Eric was delighted to see me move freely and without pain.

Molly continued her gentle persuasion, 'Nancy, ask the Father for the fullness of the Holy Spirit in your life. You know He delights to give His children good gifts.'*

So shortly after the healing of my back we invited these friends and another couple over for the evening. I wanted the Holy Spirit to be released fully into my life, that same Spirit which had taken up residence when I became a Christian.

God just needed my permission to carry out His promise and pour forth His Spirit like water on a dry and thirsty life; and He did! Our friends laid hands on me and prayed. No bells rang, there were no fireworks, but I sensed His presence and love in an indescribable new and living way.*

In the weeks that followed He made the Bible come alive and I understood clearly things I had not realized before. Jesus himself had to be baptised by the Holy Spirit there in the River Jordan; He too had no public ministry until He received power from on high. If He, who was God, perfect and sinless needed to be filled with the Spirit, how much more did I. It was no 'second blessing' but only an essential part of the fullness of all Christ desired to give. He desired to be all that was needed in my life; power, love, joy, patience and so much more. 'In Christ dwell all the riches of glory.'

It was an increased dimension and experience of the Lord Jesus Himself that the Father wanted me to have. He just needed the freedom to fill my life. There came a new ability to relax in the Lord and let Him be my patience rather than trying to be patient myself. That had been tiring! This freed me from trying to DO what He wanted to BE, what He wanted.

The Spirit's job is to reveal Jesus and lead us into truth. He began doing this in wonderful ways.* Now I

s.c.—5

began to see the fuller richness the word salvation contained; it meant not only forgiveness but health and wholeness for every area of life. What a big task He had in store to accomplish this in me! He began nudging me to open areas for Him to touch in His powerful but gentle way and release me into further wholeness and provide me with the peace, patience or gentleness that I lacked. I certainly lacked! This stubborn, self-willed, strong minded, proud lady had a lot that needed changing!

Still, I knew God loved me as I WAS; not as I might manage to make myself become. He saw me as already complete in Christ. He knew my potential and my failures. He knew that my weaknesses could become strengths. It was a continuing deep work that would go on for the rest of my lifetime. He wanted me to abide in Him and walk in all the power of the Spirit and in victory. Those deep longings of my heart for more of the Lord were being met: what joy.

I longed for Eric to experience this too. 'Dear, why don't you ask for the Holy Spirit to fill you?'

'Nan, I'm glad to see the change in you. None of the fine Christians who influenced me had this, so why do I need it?'

So my dear husband watched from afar, not against what was happening; apparently having no desire for more himself. Then, one by one, he heard that those whose lives he so admired had received the fullness of the Spirit! The Hound of Heaven was on his trail.

At that time Jean's small hands were covered by warts and one night when she was asleep I prayed for her and then forgot it. A couple of weeks later Eric noted with surprise that her hands were completely clear. We praised God for another confirmation, even in this small way, of His care as a loving Father for one of His little children. Later He healed her of a high temperature in a matter of minutes as she sat on my lap and we prayed for her.

Other times He didn't heal when we asked just as

trustingly. We didn't know why but knew we must keep our eyes on Jesus, the Healer, not on the healings; on the Giver, not the gifts.

One day when I was very ill with a high fever and pain, we prayed but saw no improvement. So we called our friends to come over and pray with us. They did and I was raised up right away the pain and fever gone. We puzzled over this.

'Why didn't the Lord heal when we prayed for this by ourselves?'

'I think perhaps God wants us all to remain dependent on others within the Body of Christ. You shouldn't be all on your own. Some things we can deal with within the family but other burdens we need to share.'

It has been evident in the years since just how vulnerable isolated groups or individuals can be. It is vital to remain part of a living church fellowship and be dependent on others. That helps to keep pride in check!*

Shortly after this I found myself in real depression which was something foreign to me even at the lowest points of my life. I woke in the morning and felt under a black cloud, with a terrible heaviness of spirit.

After suffering a few days of this I again went to our friend Martin and his wife and asked them to pray with me. They laid hands on me and asked the Lord to minister to me. The heaviness left immediately and to our wonder we realized God had done a unique thing.

He had left a perfume, a lovely fragrance, on my hair where my friends laid their hands. They assured me that they had not put anything on, it was the Lord's doing. It apparently came while we were praying.

I went home with a tremendous sense of wonder and Eric could smell the perfume as well. We were amazed at what God had done. The fragrance stayed with me for several days and other friends caught its lovely aroma also. How and why He did this I do not know. I just accepted it as a loving gift from a God who wants to give us more than we can ask or think.* '. . . your God has anointed you . . . with oil, the token of joy.'*

After a few months of watching from a distance Eric asked the Lord for the fullness of the Holy Spirit in his own life. While we were attending a Fountain Trust Conference at Ashburnham he stayed behind after one of the meetings and asked for prayer. He returned shining with joy!* The following days showed a beautiful deepening of his relationship with Christ.

At this conference we also had our first evidence of inner healing. For the previous few years Andrew had shown some anxiety when both of us went out for the evening. In one of the teaching sessions we talked about healing of the memories, especially ones related to early childhood. I became aware that this anxiety in Andrew's life must be due to having been left alone in hospital when he was an infant and then as a young child. Jeanne Harper showed us how to pray, and she suggested for children, to do this while they were asleep.

That evening in the tent, Eric and I knelt by our sleeping son and asked the Lord to heal. We prayed out loud but quietly.

'Andrew, you were never left alone there in the hospital. Jesus was always with you, even though you did not know it. Jesus was with you, you were never alone.'

From that time, and with that simple prayer, there was never any trace of anxiety in his life.

From the experiences of others we learned that for some it could take more than one prayer; it might need to be done every day for several months until complete healing was evident.

Did my other son need this inner healing to heal the effects of our separation? My thoughts often turned to him and I was aware of that ache, like a black hole in my heart. It was an emptiness, a numbness, a death that could never be properly mourned since I had to act as though nothing had happened. Inside I wept over the loss.

No one else, of course, knew this and mercifully I was not affected to a greater extent by my grief. I realized that the Lord knew about it, understood it and helped me to endure. I had to be vigilant and not dwell on it but give it to the Lord to bear.

My son was a teenager now but what was he like? Was he having difficulties? 'Lord just keep hold of him.'

I began to pray regularly over both Andrew and Jean at night, when they were asleep and ask for forgiveness in any way I had failed them. I asked Him to wipe out the effects my own sin and mistakes might have produced in them. I also made a point of apologizing to them when I had been wrong or impatient with them.

We felt a real need to invest time and energy in their lives as God had entrusted them into our care. The house echoed to the sounds of their laughter and play; we had many good times together as a family; camping, enjoying walks in the woods nearby and drives in the countryside. Friends were often there to stay or we would travel to see them. It was an enjoyable, busy life made up of the normal humdrum daily tasks. The garment of my life was drab but brightened by many patches of joy.

We sought to teach Andrew and Jean, by example, the delights of knowing God in a personal way and they came to trust in Christ while still young. He was a natural part of mine and Eric's lives and He became so for them also. Although my real interest was in my family I did enjoy working two nights a week in a small maternity hospital and was secretly surprised it wasn't painful to care for the little babies. Obviously I had buried the pain of my lost son so deeply I was not often conscious of it hurting.

We had been in England just three years when Eric applied for a teaching job in Canada. We had long wanted to move there but had been told there were no openings for teachers, like Eric, who did not have formal teachers' training. We had looked for jobs there for several months but had met a blank wall.

Eric went for his interview and on his return I ran excitedly to the door to greet him. 'Are we going?'

'Nan, I'm being pushed into a snap decision and I

can't accept the job in such a hurry. You know I've always said, God may do things quickly but not in a rush. If we are meant to go, another job will turn up.'

I felt crushed. We were all very disappointed but after a while were able to accept his decision. Years ago I learned to really work at being content in whatever situation I found myself.

A couple of weeks later the phrase, 'the Lord will give you the desires of your heart' came to mind. I wasn't even sure that it was in the Bible but after a search I found it was Psalm 37. 'Trust in the Lord, depend on Him and He will give you your hearts desire.'

This brought real peace; we wanted to go to Canada but we could safely leave it in God's hands and He would open the way if we were meant to go. In spite of the sparse job market we were at peace.

Within a few weeks we had another offer of a job with the same school and this time there was no rush. Eric accepted the position and we prepared once again to pull up roots and resettle. This was like when we left Kenya; it meant leaving dear friends and this made us sad. In some ways we wanted to remain where we were but the longing to go was stronger.

Andrew and Jean were eager with the thought of new adventures. The previous year we had been back to Minnesota to see my parents. We had taken a very enjoyable canoe trip then and it had whetted our appetite for more. I knew how much I personally missed the lovely North Country. It would also be within commuting distance of my family – only 1000 miles away!

The Canadian High Commission informed us it would take many months for us to become landed immigrants but we went ahead and put our house and car up for sale and just two months later we had all the necessary documents. In the trial and frustrations of moving we proved the true value of good friends as they helped feed us and squash the last items into the crates.

Once again we were at Heathrow Airport. There had

been many times of coming and going through here since that memorable time we first left for Africa.

So much had happened in the past three and a half years; I'd never dreamed the Lord would do so much in our lives. My eyes rested on our two children and saw the excitement in their faces and sensed it in myself also but it was well masked by exhaustion. Eric looked a bit harried having just dealt with a problem about our excess baggage but I knew he would soon be his usual calm self.

What lay ahead of us in Canada? We didn't know the future but we knew the One going with us and He was faithful and worthy to be trusted.

9: God Will Carry Us

Trust in the Lord and do good,
settle in the land and find safe pasture.
Depend upon the Lord,
and He will grant you your hearts desire.
Commit your life to the Lord;
trust in Him and He will act.
Wait quietly for the Lord,
be patient until He comes.
Psalm 37:3–5, 7

May the peace of Christ profoundly disturb us to
change into what He wants us to be.

The December dusk was just falling as our plane touched
down at Toronto International Airport: we were in
Canada. Here to welcome us, strangely enough, was Jim
the same friend of Eric's who ten years earlier greeted
us at Nairobi Airport. He was now teaching in Toronto.

We squeezed ourselves and the mountain of luggage
into his car and drove along the freeway thronged with
traffic and ringed with Christmas lights. This was very
different from that other drive from Nairobi; this time
there were no bright flowers and the temperature was
considerably lower. For me this move was a 'coming
home', back on this side of the Atlantic.

The Lord used others to help us find an apartment
and car. In a city of over two and a half million one
of our primary tasks was to find Christian fellowship;
especially a local church. We went to a couple of different
ones on the recommendation of friends and then found

the one where we felt comfortable. We realized we would never find a perfect church, since none of those exist; but we wanted one that preached Jesus and where our two children would get good grounding in the things of the Lord.

Eric began his teaching and it was a challenge to change curriculum and find his way around a new school. He also found it an interesting experience teaching girls for the first time!

Andrew and Jean settled down in their local school, found new friends and began new activities, hockey, ballet and swimming.

We knew there would be difficulties ahead in a material sense, for living was very expensive in Toronto. In spite of that, we knew we were in the will of God. It was a challenge to see how far the money would stretch and prove the truth of the old saying, 'necessity is the mother of invention'. This was a challenge to see how I could decorate, cook and sew for very little. We never lacked, God provided for all our needs.

We guarded our closeness as a family; with the upheaval of a move I made it a point to be at home when Andrew and Jean came in from school and avoided almost all evening meetings. My place was at home to give the stability of just being there. This wasn't a chore as I enjoyed the company of my family.

If our faith was true it had to be seen in practical terms around the house; worked out in the context of everyday family life. The joy and peace and patience had to work at home with the pressures there if it was to work at all. So often we failed.

It meant being honest and seeing where we went wrong but not concentrating on failures; accepting ourselves as we were but also having a desire to be more like the Lord. I tried to remember that God sees exactly what we are like and still loves us! It meant respecting myself in spite of all my faults. God wasn't finished with me yet! 'Forget what lies behind, press on to what lies ahead.'* This truth was especially pertinent for me because I wanted to enjoy our two children and forget the hurt from the past. My faith was no escape from life's difficulties but a means of working through them with joy and humour.

Even within the large city we found lots to interest us as a family; walks, bike rides and cross-country skiing, skating and tobogganing in the winter. We took advantage of a park system that stretched for miles, right at our doorstep. Here in the heart of the big city we still had wild life: racoons, rabbits and foxes.

We particularly enjoyed the times we spent camping in one of Ontario's abundance of suitable spots. Algonquin Park, about 180 miles north of us, was a favourite. Here was the beautiful Shield country; that lovely combination of rocks, trees and lakes. One autumn we spent a weekend there which was especially peaceful since the summer crowds were gone. Gone too was the summer warmth but to compensate for this was the clarity of the air; crisp with the scent of wood smoke, leaves and the soft clean smell of the pines.

That evening, as we sat around the campfire, we heard, faintly at first, a distant howling unlike anything we had heard before.

'What's that?' Andrew asked, sitting up excitedly; his beloved fire tending momentarily forgotten.

'It's the wolf pack,' our friends informed us, 'they are calling to each other. Let's try and imitate them and they will respond to us.'

We tried our best and were soon rewarded with a mournful howl in return. We really felt then we were in the true North. Later in the evening one of the wolves paid us a visit. I was putting food away and saw a form come up and grab the garbage; for a moment I thought it was just a dog! It was exciting to be so close to such beautiful, wild creatures.

Those times in the 'out-of-doors' were times of healing for me. I was not consciously aware this was happening but over the years knew how much I needed just to get out and away in the beauty of nature. It was health for my soul; the Lord used it to touch me and heal the emotional scars.

Often in the city when I saw problem teenagers my mind went to my son, almost out of his teens.

'Lord spare him from the difficulties these young people have.'

I prayed he might have the home life necessary to cause him to grow into a useful man, and come to know Jesus. Some days I was more acutely aware of my hurt and would beg Him to take away the pain at the very depths of my being. And it would soon go. Life would go on, no one aware of the agony I'd just passed through.

I read articles from time to time about reunions between children and their birth parents and felt afraid that my son might turn up on my doorstep some day. I was fearful for the distress this might produce as neither Eric, nor anyone else, knew of his existence.

'Lord, protect me from that. Somehow and someday, when I'm face to face with you in heaven, I know you will work out everything.'

Eric would know and understand and I would see my son. How wonderful that would be! It gave me a great sense of peace to know it was in God's hands. Times with others in praise and worship were helpful, and looking back I see they were another of the Lord's means of healing for me.

One such group was a monthly ladies' meeting held in Betty Madsen's home. The reflection of the Lord Jesus in her life and that of her daughters was such an encouragement to me and so many others who came into contact with them.

The group supported me to believe the Lord for healing when my doctor advised me to have major surgery. I asked him to wait a while and somehow felt convinced this time God would deal with the problem. I had been through major surgery several times over the years and wanted to avoid it if possible but knew God often heals through the surgeon's hands. It took several months before the healing was complete and my doctor agreed the surgery was no longer needed.

Slowly over these years the Lord taught me to be alert, to listen. This was hard as I am stubborn and so often unwilling to listen to others and barge ahead without thinking.

'Lord, is that for me? Did I need that word of rebuke? Was that pride?'

Gently, He put His finger on the area He wanted changed and made it clear that I must deal with it. Slowly, I noticed my critical biting comments came less frequently and there was change in other areas also.

God never points an accusing finger at us. He brings us an awareness of sin, of how we grieve Him, but whenever this happens there is with it the continuing reassurance of His deep love.

I knew the Lord was hurt when I was selfish, rude or rebellious but He was always waiting with open arms for me to ask forgiveness and change my ways. He wanted me to live a life of victory, not burdened with my failure or grief but filled with His joy and peace.

In Toronto, as in England, our lives were enriched by the fellowship we had with a wide variety of believers. God is a God of variety and we have learned a lot from others when together we worship Jesus. We took some courses from the Catholic Charismatics and found great love for Jesus and real depth in their teaching. Father Montague shared with us an important truth; at one point in his life he recognized that his anger was all he had to offer to God.

I came to see that the Lord, who knows us completely, wants us to come to Him with our real feelings and not put on a 'mask' and pretend that we feel good. We usually try and tell Him what we think we SHOULD feel not what we actually DO. This truth helped me to be more open before the Lord and feel secure knowing He accepts me as I am and as I feel right now.

Still, He is always patiently trying to lead me into further conformity with Himself. It's a continuing process of 'Becoming'. Of course God sees my bad side; He sees my need of His love and loves me enough to forgive me. I can relax. God knows all about me. I must love Him and walk in His ways; He will work out the rest. I'm free to be me and know He still loves me.

After three years of living in our apartment we found a simple semi on a quiet street; built of brick and very much like the one we had in Bristol. We liked it because it was surrounded by trees and still close to the parks.

Life was busy with involvement in the girls' group at our church as well as with a Christian diet group. We tried to reach out in a small way through TEAR Fund and World Vision. We also began to counsel, by telephone, at a local Christian television programme.

'100 Huntley Street', a daily TV programme, is broadcast across Canada and the USA. There are telephone counsellors available twenty-four hours a day for those who need encouragement or want prayer for themselves or others.

My time there, usually once a week, was a time of encouragement for me. Thankfully God doesn't wait to use me until I am completely whole or perfect; He just wants me available, flawed as I am.

On one of our usual Sunday afternoon walks Eric and I were strolling along hand in hand in the park nearby. We enjoyed walking in the autumn with the leaves thick on the ground. It is my favourite season, one that touches all the senses.

Red, gold, brown leaves sent up their familiar woodsy scent as we crunched through them. Their crisp rustling sound brought me new pleasure each fall.

Eric's words interrupted my concentration. 'It's a good weekend for the retreat.'

Andrew and Jean were at a ISCF (the high school arm of IVF) meetings all day.

'They'll have a great time catching up on all the news from their friends from camp. And if Lisa is there they won't stop laughing. Isn't it nice they get to know so many others from all over Ontario?' I said.

'Did I tell you we had a new fellow at our meeting on Thursday?'

'No you didn't. Who was it?' Eric was the staff sponsor of the group at his school.

He squeezed my hand and said, 'It's interesting both our children are involved like we were in the group. That's where I met you; the girl who wanted a man!'

What wonderful memories we had to look back to and laugh over together.

We became involved with Ontario Pioneer Camp north of Toronto. Hundreds of children and teenagers come to it during the year and I had the opportunity once again to be camp nurse during the summer and tend to my share of cuts and bruises. Our own children were there as campers and then junior counsellors. They also went on a number of canoe trips; Andrew on a 400 mile one in northern Ontario and both enjoyed the thrill of white water canoeing. As for me, I like my water flat and still!

At the beginning of our time in Canada the Lord allowed me to go through a real 'wilderness' experience; a 'dark night of the soul' as some have described it. This lasted a few years and was a very dry time spiritually when there was no real feeling of the Lord's presence. I knew He was with me even though He seemed so distant and hung on to His promise, 'I will never leave you or forsake you.'*

Regular fellowship with other Christians was necessary as well as rooting out any sin and doggedly I chose to believe He was with me even though I had no sense of this. God allowed it for my good so that I might learn to walk by faith, to trust Him and not my feelings.

He taught me the difficult lesson of walking the path of praise and choosing to do so when I felt least like it.* Listening to records of praise became a large part of my protection against discouragement and defeat. This and regular meditation on His Word allowed me to go through the years with victory. God gave it, I didn't earn it.

He took away all the external supports in order to leave me dependent on Himself alone. For all the enjoyable things we did I really didn't like being in Toronto. It was so huge; I longed to live elsewhere and tantalizing offers of jobs for Eric outside the city came and went. Friends moved away. I felt so desperately alone at times. I didn't want to tell Eric just how miserable I felt as he was trying to make a decision about the jobs and I didn't want to influence this decision. The Lord had me in a corner.

Finally I was able to relinquish my will and was willing to stay if that was where He wanted us. Surprisingly, it was not long before I was no longer resentful of the huge city and Eric found a new and better teaching job, still in Toronto and our good friends moved back. I'm so glad my foundations were laid carefully; He kept me solid on the Rock when the waves pounded hard over several years.

During this time I came across an article in Renewal Magazine. It said we often resist the touch of God in our lives; we try to escape from difficult or uncomfortable circumstances which are meant to make us turn to God. Instead we become busy, put on the radio or TV, run to friends to talk, overwork or even resort to drugs or alcohol to stop the uncomfortable feelings. It is painful but absolutely necessary to acknowledge we are hurting, angry or whatever. He wants to use those difficult things to make Himself more real to us. He did for me.

Life went on, the external ordinariness of it a contrast to the internal struggles. In some ways the hurt I felt inside became more intense but without depression. The pain was deep but usually brief and I knew Jesus' arms of love enfolded me.

I learned much during these difficult years that could not have been learned in any other way. It had long been the desire of my heart to know the Lord in a deeper way and He gives us the desires of our hearts!*

There were times over a period of several years when, with great clarity, a sense of desolation would sweep over me and for a few moments it would be almost overwhelming. It seemed to me that I was somehow catching a faint echo of the complete desolation the Lord Himself experienced as He hung on the cross and as He bore our sin and was temporarily cut off from the presence of His Father. We will never know what that was like but at times I think He calls us to share in His sufferings; to experience in different ways a tiny reflection of His intense suffering on our behalf. It is a privilege that He chooses to give us.

'All I care for is to know Christ, to experience the power of His resurrection, and to share His sufferings.'*

It usually came to mind that some of these feelings of desolation were probably rooted in my childhood or the trauma of giving up my child. Whatever the source the grief was enormous but from my earlier experiences I knew these inner hurts could be healed just as my physical ones had been.

Since Jesus is Lord of all time He can touch the events of our past with healing.* This is not always accomplished quickly as the roots are deep. It was helpful to have Eric pray with me but I was never able to share with him about my son and the accompanying feelings of bereavement. I always felt it would cause him too much pain and so I said nothing.

In spite of this the Lord enabled me generally to be a happy person, the grief only running through as a minor chord. Eric was a wonderful husband and it was relaxing knowing I didn't have to earn his love. Our family had a great sense of humour and our life in almost all its respects was one of joy and this was healing for me. He has said, 'laughter is like a good medicine'.*

I enjoyed my family, rewarding counselling work at '100 Huntley Street' and an interesting part-time job as an occupational health nurse. I took over for the usual nurses when they were away and worked both in heavy industrial plants as well as the offices of the city's large banks. My job gave me time to talk with those who came in and helped them evaluate their lifestyles. Usually it involved simply the giving of medicine for a minor ache or pain but sometimes dealing with major emotional problems or a sudden heart attack.

In our marriage the mutual commitment to love each other smoothed the meshing of two strong willed individuals. We knew one personality in a marriage should not be squashed; we must remain true to who we were, each of us developing to our fullest but within guidelines set by the Lord. We had to treasure each other and be faithful and loving, but not play a role; that of 'husband' or 'wife'.

We realized a fulfilling, happy marriage couldn't be achieved by following a formula, such as, 'Five Steps to Better Marriage', but by each of us daily drawing close to Christ.

I could never play a role as a subservient, 'yes dear' kind of wife; but in my heart, long ago, realized I must submit to Eric's final authority in order for things to work out smoothly. It was because the Lord asked this of me; Eric had no right to demand it, only the Lord could.

When we faced decisions it did not preclude a full airing of both our views, fears, or objections but God knew the intent of my heart to be the wife HE desired me to be. I often failed but went on trying.

Eric has always tried to be the husband the Lord wanted, not focussing on being the ruler in the home. He too failed; he wasn't perfect! But I found him to be a reliable shelter for me, a tower of strength, stability and protection for the whole family. His vocal, visible love, and his small kindnesses always made me deeply grateful.

In spite of this we did have times of hurt and insensitivity and there was the tendency to drift into taking each other for granted; this hurt me deeply when we let it happen. We needed to constantly re-establish our closeness and one of the means used was Marriage Encounter.

That weekend away helped us focus on effective

communication and establish a new dialogue with each other. We took the time and effort to keep our love alive. It was a tremendous time and we found a new sense of wonder at the love He had given us for each other.

During the weekend the question stared up at me from the paper and released a flood of emotions. 'What is your most painful memory that you are unable to share? How does that make you feel?'

That gave me an intense desire to tell Eric. Here was the safest and best opportunity to let Eric know about my lost child. I hesitated but could not go through with it and risk hurting him and so I missed the chance to get rid of this secret in the warm atmosphere which that special weekend produced.

I looked back and realized that God knew what sort of husband I needed; one to love me unreservedly and who would take pains to express that love. There was peace in our home and our teenagers were a source of real pleasure and delight, we loved them deeply. My wants were not all satisfied but my needs certainly were and I treasured my spiritual riches.

What more could I want? After almost nine years in Canada life was full of the ordinary, the mundane but necessary tasks; shopping, washing and ironing, making beds, cleaning and endless piles of dishes. I frequently tried new crafts and enjoyed learning new skills; life was good. But at times my heart ached for he, WHOM, I did not have.

The spring of 1983 was exceptionally late and the cool weather had lingered but now it was beginning to be more like summer. We had planted the garden and soon the flowers would be blooming and our own fresh vegetables would be available.

Early in May I sat there in my soft comfortable chair, the sun streaming through the living room window; the warmth of it enveloped me and our cat curled up next to me. My eyes were drawn to our big ash tree clothed now in its new coat of green and a few late tulips which

gave a dash of red. The magnolia with its pretty cups of
pale pink was nodding in the breeze.

'Lord you have given me so much. You have taught
me so many things, let me share more of it with others.'

10: The Phone Call

'. . . always in life there is a place to leave and a new
place to find and in between a zone of hesitation
and uncertainty tinged with more or less intense
anxiety. It shows itself at critical turning points in
our life. We need support to live but need also at
some point to let go and grasp a new support. The
middle is a zone of anxiety . . . a supportless zone.

There is always a letting go of what we have acquired
and acquiring what we did not possess. We leave
one place to find another; we turn back on the past
to go forward toward the future.'
Paul Tournier, *A Place for You*

The familiar ringing of the phone interrupted my work
in the kitchen. I set the tray of freshly baked cookies on
the counter and went to answer it. 'Who can it be this
time?' I thought.

The voice was pleasant but unfamiliar. 'Am I speaking
to Nancy Moore?'

'Yes, can I help you?'

After my affirmative response came another surprise, a
request for my maiden name. Then the caller introduced
herself.

'I'm Meg Bale, a social worker in Minneapolis,' and
more staggering questions followed.

'Did you have a son, born in Minneapolis in 1956?'

My mind had suddenly gone numb but I was able to
respond hesitatingly, 'Yes . . . I did. Why do you ask?'

'He would like to get in touch with you. Are you willing?'

My comfortable, ordered life was in the space of a few seconds, threatened with collapse. All that was precious to me in my family, my friends, my way of life was now at risk, and my mind raced through the possibilities at a speed I could not have imagined. Feelings of fear, shock and also of tremendous relief clamoured for attention.

Was I dreaming? I couldn't have heard her correctly. How could this be happening after all this time? Now I knew that my son was alive. There had been no news of him for 27 years. Oh, at last to have word after so long.

He was alive but what was he like? Where was he now? Why did he want to get in touch with me after so long? What would happen next? Neither my husband nor my children were aware of this boy's, no, man's existence. No one knew. What was I to do? I didn't want to hurt them. They must not know or they might be deeply offended that they hadn't known before. Above all, how would Eric feel because I had not told him years ago?

The kindly voice interrupted these conflicting thoughts racing through my mind. 'Your son, Tom, doesn't want to disrupt or interfere in your life in any way. He just wants to make contact with you. Do you want that? Would this be possible?'

'Yes.' I realized immediately that I could not appear to reject him a second time. I had been forced, through much agony, to give him up those many years ago and now I must not stop this gesture on his part.

'Tom wants to reassure you he is alright. He is happily married and has two young sons. He enjoys his job as a supervisor, working with heavy equipment. But he would especially like some information from you about his background.

'He looks like a nice, and I might add a very handsome man from the picture I have of him. I'll send you his letter and the photograph right away.'

s.c.—6

We spoke for a long time as I tried to let her know why I had to release him for adoption and then what had happened in my life since his birth. I knew she would relay this information on to him.

'I will certainly respond to him but can't keep up a long correspondence as my husband is unaware of Tom's existence. Our relationship is very close and special to me and I don't want to damage it nor go behind his back.'

'I understand; it must be difficult for you,' she said.

'If I suddenly say something now after all these years, it might be extremely painful. I know my husband's love won't change but he might be hurt and I don't want that to happen. I certainly will write to Tom even though there can't be a relationship which can continue.'

'I will send his letter right away and you can be assured your privacy will be protected. You can correspond through me at the agency.'

The phone call was over. It lasted almost half an hour but time had stood still. I rushed upstairs and knelt by our bed. I was in tears and turmoil and I cried out to the Lord to keep control of all this. I stayed there for some minutes but realized the family was due home anytime. No one must find me crying or upset.

I got up and tried to compose myself to control the intense emotions racing through me. Relief and fear vied for attention. I went back downstairs and began to make supper as though nothing had happened but my mind was in a state of shock. In a matter of a few moments the whole course of my life had changed forever.

I heard the car pull up outside and the family came in. 'Have a good day?' Eric asked as he gave me a kiss. I replied affirmatively but in a non-committal way. I dared not express my distress, so I involved myself peeling potatoes and the rest of supper preparations.

We sat down around the table; Jean and Andrew and Eric chatting about their days at school. Everything was the same and yet everything was absolutely changed. I finally had to face the past afresh and respond to my son. But this present life was so precious to me. Could I sacrifice it all?

To all outward appearances everything was normal about the house that evening. No one was aware that anything unusual had happened to me, neither then nor in the days ahead. Life went on normally but inside I was distraught and in constant prayer to the Lord for help and guidance. What was I to do? At least I knew WHOM to turn to for help this time.

Those days following the fateful phone call were difficult ones. I was in unprecedented inner agony. It was like being on a runaway horse that was out of control.

'Keep hold of everything Lord. I praise you and give the whole situation to you. Just hang on to me through all of this.'*

I was upheld in those days by praise. Travelling back and forth to work I played a tape of praise songs and made them my prayer and plea. There was nothing, no one to give me advice and nowhere to turn except to Jesus.*

I had to keep my concentration on Him or the dread of what would happen came rushing in like a river in flood. The Lord was the only one who could keep my life from coming apart. It was so easy to get tangled in the events and emotions surging around and within me. It was necessary to force myself to focus attention on Jesus by praise and worship. At times, when words and tears were not enough, I prayed in the Spirit. It was the only way to get beyond the limits of my own words and thoughts and allow the Holy Spirit to pray through me.*

There was an intense longing to share all of this with Eric but I was fearful of the trouble it might cause. I did not want to inflict this on him as I loved him deeply.

After what seemed like an eternity, in reality it was only a week, the picture and letter from my son Tom arrived.

I ripped open the envelope with trembling hands and then my heart stood still as I saw, not a child now, but a grown man. What a relief to have this word from him after 27 years! I stared for ages at that picture. It was a tremendous sense of joy to see him after so many grieving years when I had no word about him. He was such a good looking man and with a very lovely wife. My son alive at last!

Tom described, very briefly, some of the events of his life and what he was now doing. I only found out later that this first letter could contain no identifying information and was therefore slightly stiff and formal.

The past became reality. So often I had wondered what had become of him. Had he become one of the hurting drop-outs who could find no happy, worthwhile place in society? Was he even alive or had he gone to Vietnam like so many young men of his age and never returned? From his letter he sounded like a normal, happy man. Somehow, he seemed kind and gentle just from his picture.

It was difficult to compose that first letter to Tom. I wanted to be sure what was written would be just right, for I knew how important it would be to him. I wanted him to know how difficult and painful it had been to relinquish him and that I had never completely recovered from the grief of that separation. He had never been forgotten.

After a lot of thought and prayer I began that important letter. . . . 'Dear Tom, It is so wonderful to know you are alright. I feel so grateful for your adoptive parents, they have obviously done a very good job in raising you.

I want you to know you were never a mistake in the Lord's eyes; He lovingly formed you and has cared for you all these years.*

Some verses from the Bible that have meant a lot to me might be a help to you too and are found in Psalm 139. It speaks of how God forms us in our mother's womb, He knows us and watches over us our whole life through. God knew you before I did and wants your love and has a plan for your life.

Over the years I have prayed for you to find the real

reason for living. I have found such joy and peace in knowing Jesus and long for you to know that too.

Since you are a grown man Tom, you already have loving parents so we cannot have a mother-son, parent-child relationship. But we can have a special friendship, a relationship based on the deep tie of our kinship.

The past is not really important. I hope you will treasure your wife and children and devote time and energy to developing a happy family life. It would be nice to keep writing but we can only exchange a letter or two as I can't risk hurting my husband. . .'

For days the battle had raged. Yes I must tell Eric; no I can't. I lay awake for long hours every night beside him as he slept peacefully, unaware of what was happening to me. The conviction grew steadily stronger; I knew the Lord was asking me to tell him, but the fear of the consequences was equally strong.

Finally I broke before the Lord, sometime in the small hours of Friday night. God was asking me to take the risk and tell Eric.

'Just trust Me.' He seemed to be saying to my heart and I knew I had to.

I would have to tell him on Sunday; it was the only time we could be sure of being alone after the evening service when our children would be going out with the other young people.

Saturday came and went with the usual activities and so did Sunday. Outwardly everything was normal but I knew that a violent storm was about to break around Eric. Our whole future depended on his reaction to the news and I wondered if I should go through with it after all? But there was the distinct feeling the Lord was pushing and prompting me to be vulnerable again. Revealing this secret would make me vulnerable as never before in our marriage. Could I do it?

We went to church that beautiful, early June evening and I was apprehensive lest someone invited us to their home afterwards: no one did. It was obvious that the time had come and there was no escape. As we drove back I was silent, praying for wisdom to tell Eric in the right way. The lilac bushes were in full bloom and Eric commented.

'Aren't they beautiful? You always enjoy them don't you?'

'Yes I do they have a lovely smell.'

I said no more and he looked across at me wonderingly, but said nothing. A minute or two later we were home and I knew how much the next few moments would affect both our lives. I had never kept secrets from him, except this one and it was a 'block buster'.

As I stood in the kitchen, making tea, my unease for the first time became apparent. I was obviously preoccupied and it caused Eric to ask, 'What's the matter dear?'

My composure was failing fast but I managed an answer, 'Eric I'm afraid you must be hurt in order for me to be healed.'

The tears started to flow and he took my hand, 'What do you mean? Come on let's sit down,' and he led me to the settee.

So this was the moment I had dreaded and yet longed for during our years together. Eric sat with his arm around me and I heard myself say, through the tears.

'A son I had, 27 years ago, wants to get in touch with me. He was born just before I went into nurses' training and I had to give him up for adoption. Nobody knew about it and I've always wanted to tell you but it just never seemed the right time.'

He didn't pull away, but held me even tighter and closer, 'Sweetheart, I love you. How have you managed to keep this to yourself all this time? That must have been the source of a lot of the hurt from the past hasn't it?'

I nodded, 'Yes it has and I so wanted to tell you.'

'What has happened? How did you hear?'

'A social worker called me ten days ago from Minneapolis and told me about him. Then she sent me a letter and photo. He's married and lives in Arizona.'

106

'Oh Nan, I'm glad you've told me, what a load you have carried alone; we should have shared it.'

'Remember when you asked me to marry you, I told you I'd been deeply hurt once and was afraid to care again?'

'Yes dear I do, I didn't pursue it as you know; if there was anything you had wanted to tell me I knew you would. I didn't have to know, it was in the past.'

'Those few days were so rushed and I kept looking for a chance to share but there was no right time. So I just felt it was a burden I would have to keep to myself.'

'Dearest, I'm so sorry you had to and wish I could have helped you to do it.'

'But how would you have reacted if I had told you then; would you have been able to accept it?'

'Well Nan, I don't know. I think I could. But it's hard to know now: I'm a different person now than I was 21 years ago.'

That was past history now, what mattered was the present and my loving husband did understand and accepted me now.*

'Did NO one know about this baby?'

'Not really, even my parents only found out when I was in labour as I was out of town working. I did ask my Pastor before we were married and he advised me to forget it and not say anything and I had to tell Dr. Mary in Nairobi but otherwise no one knew. So really no one knew.'

'Well, have you replied to his letter?

'Yes, I said I couldn't keep up any correspondence, because you didn't know.'

'Well I do now, and you don't have to bear any of this on your own any longer.'

Eric kissed me and held me closer as the tears flowed again. 'It's alright, you need to cry.'

And I did. The relief surged through me as I shared this for the first time with my loving husband; he was not condemning me. He accepted me as I was and loved me. He wasn't hurt. That which I had always feared would happen, hadn't. We prayed for the Lord to heal the painful memories from the past and for wisdom in dealing with this new situation.

Then Eric laughed and I looked up in surprise as I asked, 'What are you laughing at?'

He replied. 'So what did you expect me to say when you told me, "Go away, I don't want anything more to do with you?" '

'I knew you wouldn't stop loving me, but I was afraid it might hurt you because I hadn't told you at the start.'

'The only pain I feel is that you have had to carry this alone for so long.'

'It wasn't alone, the Lord took a lot away.'

'Yes, but you have gone through so much even so!' And I had. The tears came as I was reminded of it all. We continued to talk and pray about this in the coming days.

It was such a relief to be able to share with Eric. What a man! Now I could write to Tom directly and give him my name and address. At this point, however, we did not feel any need to tell our two children all this. It seemed it ought to be limited to ourselves and Tom.

'Do you want to see your son?' Eric asked me.

'I don't know, I guess someday we could meet but when could that be? He lives so far away.'

My heart, although relieved at contact, was still quite numb as far as any feelings towards Tom. It is impossible to immediately turn feelings on after completely suppressing them for 27 years. The suppression of sorrow as well as love had been so effective that there had to be a gradual thawing out and opening up of my heart over the next days.

Now I wrote to Meg Bale and let her know my husband had been told and I was enclosing a letter to Tom which had my name and address in it. She immediately called Tom with the news and he was overjoyed. He had been happy enough with any news at all from me and this was far more than he had hoped for.

A few days later Eric and I sat in our front yard

reading a second letter from Tom. I was touched deeply as I read of his joy at being able to write directly.

'Nancy, I'm so thrilled that we are in touch at last and I can write directly to you. Thank you for the first letter you wrote; it was better than I ever dreamed possible. I'm sorry for the hurt you have had over the years. I want you to know how much I care for you and have always felt you cared for me all these years.'

I read further and could hardly believe my eyes, it was too good to be true.

'Nancy it's wonderful to know you are a Christian too.'

Tom also knew Jesus personally! I sat there simply overwhelmed by joy! I was overcome by the love and mercy of God for having kept His hand on Tom. Tears of gratitude flowed as I sensed what a marvellous and unexpected gift God was giving me.

I handed Eric the letter to read and his eyes shone as he looked over at me and smiled. We rejoiced together and he sensed just how moving this was for me; my son had found new life in Jesus. God delights to give good gifts to us, His beloved children.

Tom went on to say, '. . . it was through my wife JoAnne, before we were married. She helped me to find a personal relationship with Jesus Christ.'

God in his providence had fitted all the pieces together into such a beautiful whole when I, myself could do nothing. Here was another bond that we had in common and this made us feel closer immediately.

Tom and I, by letter, and by telephone began to put together the pieces of the years apart. I was deeply touched by Tom's love and concern for me. He didn't want to cause any hurt or interfere in my life.

In our first phone call he simply said, 'I love you. You are very special to me.'

I could hardly talk as I was overcome by the fact he could care for me, even though I had to give him up. It was an overwhelming feeling, such a kind and caring son the Lord had given back. I could hardly believe it was happening to me and the 'happy tears' came unprompted, then, and often during those weeks.

Tom wrote again and said, 'I've always wanted to find you Nancy, ever since I have been a teenager. I had a happy childhood with my adoptive parents and three sisters, born after I was adopted. But the desire to search became especially strong when my first son was born. When I took Joshua in my arms it was an indescribable feeling, it was a very moving and emotional experience. For the first time I was able to see and hold someone who was related to me. He was someone who was my own flesh and blood, someone like me in a way no one else was and I thanked God for giving him to JoAnne and me.

This only increased my determination to search for you. It was three years before the search could begin, and two more before it was completed. In the beginning I was a bit afraid; what would I find? As I prayed about it there was the growing feeling I would like whatever I found. And I do, I'm so glad I found you!'

We both realised we very much wanted to meet, and soon; the need to see each other grew by the day. It was hard to believe how the Lord was awakening in my heart a deep love which before I had never dared allow myself to feel towards this son. I had known that if I had let myself love him fully I could not have coped, so I had pushed down, deep into my subconscious, all my feelings of love for him. At infrequent intervals over the years they had surfaced, as great feelings of grief and desolation that I could hardly bear.

Now this had all changed. My night was turned into day! My son was alive and was such a gentle sensitive man. The joy of this was unlike anything I had ever experienced. It was a time of great emotional upheaval and I knew the extremes, the agony and the ecstasy. There were times of intense joy mixed with periods when the suppressed emotions of the past came to the surface needing to be healed. Eric and I prayed specifically for them and the Lord touched them.

Our desire for a meeting was discussed and various possibilities were examined. Eric came home one day and found me upset.

'What's the matter dear, has something happened?'

'I just feel so discouraged. How can we possibly get to see Tom?'

'Why not?'

'It's so far, over 2500 miles, and that will cost so much. It's too expensive, we simply can't afford it.'

'That's not like you to talk that way. You can't stop now so close to meeting Tom at last. We can work something out.'

I soon realized I was not acting in faith but just trying to reason things through with my own understanding. And it produced the inevitable consequences, confusion and discouragement.

As soon as I stopped trying to figure it all out and manage it on my own and once more gave it to the Lord to arrange, things began to fall into place. We would pool our resources and Tom and JoAnne and the children would fly to Toronto. Plans went smoothly from there on and there was no more discouragement. I learned an invaluable lesson on the necessity of operating by faith.

Days seemed to drag as they do when a keenly anticipated event is upcoming but fortunately I was busy working full-time. It helped keep me occupied as I was camp nurse for two more weeks. If only the days would hurry.

'Nan are you anxious at all about meeting Tom?'

'Oh no, not in the least. I just feel overwhelming jubilation and as if I might burst with joy!'

There certainly was no room for doubt or worry. Tom wrote and said he too was feeling exactly the same.

It seemed fitting that this first meeting should involve only Tom, his wife JoAnne, Eric and myself. Our two teenagers were away for most of the summer, Andrew on a mission team in Alaska and Jean at Pioneer Camp. Their meeting with Tom would come later, for we had come to recognise they could not be excluded from this widening circle of joy. How could I have ever thought differently? But I had and that was only weeks ago!

11: Overwhelmed By Joy

For this son of mine was dead
and has come back to life;
he was lost and is found.

And the festivities began.
Luke 15:23–24

. . . a joy too great for words. . .
1 Peter 1:8

This was the day! Tom, JoAnne and their two children
were due to arrive on the late evening plane. It hardly
seemed possible and yet it was actually happening; I
would see my son for the first time in 27 years! How I
longed to see him in person and give him a big hug.

The day dragged by on leaden feet and although I can
often be oblivious to time, I was aware of every minute,
10:30 just didn't seem to get any closer. The house was
ready; neat and tidy. First impressions were important
and I wanted our home to be pleasant and inviting.

Surely I'll burst with excitement, I thought. At last I
would see Tom and talk with him face to face. How
good it would be to also meet his wife and young sons.
There was so much catching up to do.

Slowly, slowly evening came and Eric and I prepared
to go to the airport. He called to confirm the arrival
time.

'Nan, they said the plane will be an hour late.'

My heart sank, it couldn't be, 'I'll never be able to
wait another hour, after all these years; I can't stand it!'

'You'll manage love; I know it's hard.' Eric came over and put his arms around me and held me close.

'I know the last few hours are the hardest. Let's just go to the airport as we planned and we can wait there.'

As we drove to the airport I didn't say much. Eric knew my emotions were impossible to put into words. I tried to contain the joy, keep it under control, but it was an impossible task. I felt as though I would explode with joy, indescribable joy! Once again I was overcome as I thought, how good God is to be working this out in such a beautiful way. It was more than I could comprehend. Tears came as they had done frequently over the past few weeks. They were tears of happiness at the completely unexpected gift God was giving me. That which had been severed was being restored in the gift of a new relationship with my son. The wonder of it was beyond believing.

We arrived at the airport and went to have a cold drink. I could scarcely swallow it, impatience and anticipation had tightened my throat. Eric knew the agony of waiting this last long hour and he held my hand tightly.

'It hardly seems possible how much our life has been changed in just two short months,' he said.

'I know and somehow I still feel like I should pinch myself; that it is all just a dream and they aren't really coming tonight.'

We sat reviewing the amazing events of the past weeks. I looked up and exclaimed, 'Flight 595 has landed. They're here!'

I had seen the plane's number flash on the arrivals board. 'We can't go down yet; they still have to come through customs and immigration.'

'For your sake Nan I hope it doesn't take them too long.'

'Do you think we'll recognize them right away? They must look like their photograph. Oh I'll recognize Tom!'

I didn't doubt that for a moment.

We went down to the arrivals gate and stood up close to the barrier. I was oblivious to the crowds of people milling around us. They were equally unaware of the tumult of emotions milling around inside of me.

There he was! At long last, just like his picture and yet so much better.

We reached across the barrier; and across the years and I was engulfed in big loving arms.

Tom was giving ME that hug! What a feeling! Better than the best dream come true! Never had I ever dared to hope for a reunion and yet here was my son, and I wasn't dreaming. God not only gave me back my son, but my daughter-in-law and my grandchildren. There were more hugs all around for JoAnne, Joshua and Troy.

'JoAnne they look just like their picture. Nancy it's so good to see you. I can't believe it's happening. You know I knew it was you right away because of the big smile on your face!'

'Tom had a similar grin the whole way here on the plane', JoAnne confided.

What joy.

We got the luggage and everyone out to the car and then I stepped back and had another good look at Tom. 'It's wonderful to see you. I still can't comprehend it even now.'

I looked up at him, trying to take in the fact – here is my son. I saw him standing there, tall and smiling down at me; dark wavy hair, a moustache, and gentle brown eyes. Tom gave me another delightful hug and then we saw in each other's eyes the love which had been kept locked inside each of us for many long years.

'I can't believe it JoAnne; he's real. We are together at last. I've wanted this for so long.'

We finally got everyone into the car and headed for home and we all tried to talk at once, there was so much to be said.

We arrived back at the house and came inside. 'Welcome home Tom.'

'It's so good to be here, but somehow it doesn't seem real.'

We soon got the children, Joshua and Troy tucked

into bed and they were soon fast asleep worn out from their long trip.

'Come tell me about yourself Tom.'

The four of us sat down in the living room and began to talk. And talk! The blank years began to take on flesh. We were completely at ease with one another. It was almost like picking up a conversation that had stopped after a gap. We felt as though we had known each other all our lives, but of course there was also a need to learn about each other.

It was wonderful just to sit and look at my son, lost to me for so many years, and see the man he had turned out to be. Tom also had the same need to stare; we needed to absorb what the other looked like. It was a delayed bonding that was being accomplished.

'You have obviously had a good home all these years,' I said looking at the gentle man sitting across from me. 'Your parents have obviously loved and cared for you well.'

'Oh yes, I've always felt loved and known I was adopted from an early age. I guess it made me feel special. But I have also wanted to be my own person and set my own path in life.'

I saw Tom liked to dress casually like myself. He had not come dressed in a suit, the weather was too hot for that. I was in my favourite red blouse and navy skirt; somehow I didn't feel it right to dress up fancy for this initial meeting. I was not out to overwhelm or impress him; just to be myself but to try and look my best. The joy of the occasion saw to that, it gave me a real glow.

Our home wasn't elaborate either, we enjoyed its modest surroundings and so I was gratified to hear Tom say, 'I feel right at home Nancy, your house is so comfortable and it even smells good.'

'Oh, that's some muffins and cookies I baked; I thought we might need something to eat later. I'm always hungry.'

'Me too!' He grinned. How alike we were.

We all experienced an instant oneness; there was no

effort to it. It was just there. There was a deep bond between us which we could not have produced ourselves. It was a conversation which didn't need many words; it was a language of the heart, a sharing of all the love and joy we felt at being together after so many years.

As we sat down to eat, the words from Luke which had been in my mind for the past few weeks came to me.

'For this son of mine was dead and has come back to life. He was lost and is found, and the festivities began.'*

My son was alive.

He whom I had grieved over all these years. My son was no longer dead; he was very much alive and actually here with us.

Joy unspeakable!

This was the biggest and best celebration I'd ever known; there was so much to be grateful for; we were celebrating our restoration to each other.

Like the father in the story of the prodigal son, I, over the years, was unable to completely enjoy my riches while my heart yearned for my lost son. I had longed to know where he was and couldn't be fully content until I could see him again.

Now I was full of joy. Joy that healed the years of hurt. We joined hands around the table and Eric gave thanks, for the food and for our reunion.

'If only Andrew and Jean could be here that would be even more wonderful.'

Yet we knew it was better for us to meet first and then have everyone get together later. I'm not sure we could have handled all the emotions at this first meeting if more had been present.

We sat around the table basking in the joy of a dream come true. Tom had found me. What I had never dared to hope for had happened.

'God has done this thing and it is wonderful in our eyes.'* He brought the broken pieces together. Tom and I were reunited. Those areas of brokenness in both our lives were being restored. We were beginning the healing and rebuilding of wonderful relationships.

Even with the restoring of this relationship between Tom and myself there was still the continuing and very close one between Tom and his adoptive parents. I knew there was a love and bond in the Rye family that nothing would change; he was a part of them and they of him.

'He puts the solitary in families.'* He did this for Tom, he had been given a family; given that which he needed to grow into the kind and loving man I now saw. I felt deeply grateful for them.

As soon as we finished eating Tom phoned his parents to say they had arrived safely and everything was going well. He wanted to put their minds at rest. They might wonder if we would get along. Would Tom feel at ease in our home and would Eric accept him? He was able to reassure them that he felt very welcomed by both of us and we were thoroughly enjoying each others' company!

It was a privilege for me to talk with his mom and dad myself.

'Thank you for helping Tom find me. He is a wonderful man and I just want you to know how grateful I feel that you could be the answer to my prayers and gave Tom such a good loving home.'

It came to me once again how amazing it was I didn't feel jealous about them. I never allowed myself to look back with longing for what 'might have been'. God allowed me to feel peace and not regret about the lost years which I was unable to have with Tom. To release him for adoption was the only decision I could make at the time; and I had had to live with that decision. It had not been easy but I was thankful for the family Tom had been given.

I was also seeing at first hand, even in those first few hours, what a wonderful son they/I had; he had the characteristics I valued in my other children. Tom's adoptive parents had been the instruments God used to help produce a kind and sensitive man.

I felt washed in a river of joy. My son was restored to

118

me; the beginning of a brand new friendship. I could not have and did not want a mother's role with Tom. He was a grown man married to a lovely wife who loved him and who was caring very well for him. Nevertheless we had a unique relationship; it created a bond we both felt deeply. A tremendous feeling of connectedness, of kinship, was there.

'You know Tom, it's important that we have met because now you can break any myths you might have carried about me; sometimes we can idolize the one we have never seen. I have lots of faults, just ask Eric. I am often bossy and nag a lot!'

'How long did you live in Minnesota before you moved to Arizona?' Eric asked.

'We moved when I was seven. I love the country down in the southwest and that's where I met Jo.'

I looked at the two of them, what a handsome couple. 'You said in your letter it was through JoAnne you became a Christian. When was that?'

'Well, I saw Tom in our high school and he was so nice, and different from the other fellows and I was determined to get to know him! And I finally got him to ask me out.'

'JoAnne took me to her church and it was there I realized I needed to know Jesus. Even though I was raised in the church I'd never responded personally.'

'Thank you JoAnne for being the means the Lord used in Tom's life.' How purposefully God had watched over my son.

Even though Eric and JoAnne did not feel all the emotions with the same intensity Tom and I felt; they happily entered into the celebration as well. They could not help but be caught up in the joy we felt.

'Eric, I appreciate how you have been so helpful to Nancy and myself through all of this. I certainly don't want to disturb your life.'

'Well Tom, your contact with Nancy has certainly disrupted our lives! But it is a wonderful thing to have happened. I can see how good it has been for her and

I'm more than happy to have you and JoAnne and the children here with us.'

'Thanks, that means a lot to me to know we are welcomed by you too.' Tom said.

'I hope the kids won't be any trouble,' JoAnne replied.

I could sense she felt a bit worried that their arrival with two children, Josh, five and Troy six months would be a bother. I reached out to pat her hand and tried to reassure her.

'I'm sure it will be an upheaval but I'm so glad you all came; and we are used to having friend's babies around. I know what it's like to travel with kids because we spent time at Eric's mothers or my parents with our two when they were small.'

The four of us could not stop talking, what a reunion! It was better than I thought it would be. It was so delightful to begin enjoying each others company. I had always appreciated Andrew and Jean's companionship and now to be given another son and daughter to enjoy was almost more than I could absorb.

We experienced real fellowship in the fullest sense of the word. Christ was at the centre of all this and we could sense that unity we had in Him. We have known this with other Christians all over the world but to have our tie of kinship made the oneness more intense.

'Nan, do you realize its 3am? You have to get some sleep before you get up for work tomorrow morning.'

My husband was concerned for me, recognizing our need to talk and yet to get the needed rest. With reluctance I agreed.

Tomorrow would be my last day of work for a while, so although we didn't want to stop talking we knew we must for at least a short time. I'm not sure if I got many minutes of sleep as I was too excited to shut my eyes.

It was difficult for me to leave them the next morning and go off to work with Tom just coming after a lifetime away. Fortunately Eric was home on holiday. Looking back I see the Lord was getting me out of the way for a few hours so they could all become closer without interference from me. They spent a good day doing carpentry work and finished off the new deck in the back yard.

That evening after supper we spent time looking at the photos Tom had brought. Now I could see the years recorded from infancy to the present. I found an amazing thing happening; I could look at these baby pictures of Tom without hurt or regret. Even though I missed this part of his life I did not feel anguish because of it. God had worked unknowingly and I only felt thankful for what God was giving me NOW. I had an immense present joy and nothing could mar it. God was giving me a new day, my son returned. I was able to enjoy today without regrets for the past.

'These are lovely wedding pictures. How old were you two when you got married?'

'I was 20 and Jo was 19. We were young but I wanted to begin a new life on our own. We wanted to build our future together.'

'And this is your mom and dad? They look like such kind people.'

'They are; I've been thankful for them and love them deeply. They have done so much for me and encouraged me in my search for you.'

'Over the years, Tom, one of the things that helped me was knowing some couple must be finding real joy in you and providing the care I couldn't. Now I know for sure that this was true, what a relief that is for me.'

'How long did it take you to find Nancy?' Eric asked.

'It was just over a year from when I began contact with the agency. We went to Minnesota and had a long interview and I got my genetic and medical background information.

'From the description they gave I knew I must look something like my birthparents. That made me feel good to know I looked like someone! It's even more wonderful to see you and see me in you.'

'Yes I know what you mean, its an indescribable feeling.'

'In your first letter Nancy, you said the past isn't important and only my adoptive family was.'

'Yes, I remember writing that but I can see I was wrong. I had no idea how important finding me could be for you.'

'I wanted to find you,' Tom said, 'and let you know I was alright and that I love you. Somehow I sensed you must be hurting and I wanted to help that and just share the Lord with you.'

I really couldn't reply as once again I was overcome by the care and concern Tom showed towards me.

It was amazing that we did not feel any awkward moments with each other; there was just so much fun. We were even relaxed enough to enjoy teasing each other. Eric and I soon became known as the 'little people' because we were short in comparison with the 'giants', Tom and his wife.

We noticed frequently how much Tom and I resembled each other and we even thought and acted alike. I watched Tom sitting there cross-legged on the floor in a position I so often adopted.

'Eric he even sits like I do and like Andrew and Jean!'

The others noticed the similarity of our personalities and ways of working. It was just like meeting a long lost twin. We thought and acted so much alike. I had been trying for years, rather unsuccessfully, to teach my teenagers to organize their work more efficiently to save time and effort.

Tom was later asked by the man at work when he returned, 'Is she like you? Does she do six jobs at the same time like you do?'!

Those days we had together sharing, talking and sightseeing were wonderful. It was delightful just to be in each others company enjoying some of the interesting things in and around Toronto. We took the fifteen minute ferry ride to Toronto Islands, at the foot of the city; here the children enjoyed the beach and we walked and talked and felt miles from the big city.

Because it was so hot we found it pleasant to go for

122

walks in the park just near our home and sit by the stream. We sat there together, a silent sharing of that enjoyment that came from just watching the water running between the smooth stones. The sun was warm on our backs and time drifted away unnoticed.

We also went to Niagara Falls and so fulfilled a long standing dream of theirs. They felt the same awe we always did as we stood at the edge of the huge cataract. The roar of the water as it slipped over the edge was heart stopping. Things are doubly enjoyable when they are shared; so it was as we stood together and watched in wonder.

The places we went to see were not the important part of this time. Rather, it was just being together enjoying the time we had, and through it healing the lost past when we we apart.

Visiting and sightseeing with a teething and wakeful baby wasn't always easy but we would not have missed it for the world. Troy's funny ways gave us much to laugh at. Fortunately Josh was old enough to enjoy things and he found Toronto's soft green grass fun to play on. It was quite unlike the dry prickly Arizona grass he was used to.

We noted the love Tom and JoAnne had for each other; that was wonderful to see; as was the tenderness Tom showed towards his sons.

'Tom you love your kids but I'm glad to see you also discipline them. Our views on raising children are very similar; we have always been firm with our two.'

'Yes, we don't like to see unruly children, they're not very nice to have around.' JoAnne said.

'Our views exactly.' Our common commitment to Christ brought so much that was alike in the way we thought and acted.

We were aware of how much Tom not only valued his wife and children but also his adopted family; family occasions were important. JoAnne told me how he spent long hours keeping his parents' and sisters' cars running and helping out in many ways. People and relationships, not possessions were important to them as they were to us.

We liked the outdoors and things of nature just as they did. We enjoyed the warm July weather as we sat out on our new back deck and discussed care of the garden and fruit trees. Together we picked our raspberries and beans and spent an afternoon wandering through the forest looking at trees, and wildflowers.

What a glorious new friendship we were establishing. It is not often we are given such instant loving friends and they were my son and daughter.

Over the years I had wanted to pray for Tom in person, to pray for any effects that may have come from our separation. This was a desire ever since I knew that God heals the wounds of the past. I had prayed for him over the years never dreaming I might ever be able to do it in person.

Now we were together and could ask God to go back over the years and heal any hurts or resentment that might be there. I had long felt an adopted person might have a deep sense of rejection. Tom didn't have any he was aware of but as we knew personally, it might be deeper and not on a conscious level. We just asked the Lord to do what was necessary. It was a privilege that Eric and I could pray for him.

We took time as well to pray for the Lord to complete the healing of the heartache at my relinquishing Tom. This I had done over the years, but now was the precious time to do it together.

I could not help crying again and I told Tom how difficult it had been to allow him to be adopted. Both of us had experienced a severing, almost a death, but a death which could never be mourned properly. Now it could be healed.

'Tom my grief over leaving you never left but God enabled me to cope. The hurt didn't go but I was given the ability to deal with it with some measure of victory. God healed a lot over the years.

It's so wonderful to be with you at last; I never

expected to ever see you again. I wish I could have loved you all through your life Tom.'

'You did.'

'What do you mean?' I asked.

'You did, you gave me life. Thank you for that. I love you.' With these words Tom gave me a loving hug!

The next day as we came out of the Sunday morning service Tom looked down at me gravely. The sermon had been on abortion.

'Praise God you didn't have one. Thank you for all the difficult times you went through for me.'

I couldn't reply, my emotions were too much to voice. What joy I might have missed!

The days flew by quickly and we realized regretfully that our time together was drawing to a close. We were having such a good time and didn't want it to end. But we knew that we were opening up a new chapter in our lives. This was only the beginning of many other good times together.

I could not stop saying, 'if only Andrew and Jean were here to enjoy this with us.'

It was echoed by Tom and JoAnne. 'We can hardly wait to meet them, they sound like a wonderful pair.'

We longed that our two might share in the tremendous joy we felt. And they would.

How thankful I was the way Eric had accepted Tom and JoAnne; yet I had never doubted he would. I could see he loved them as much as I did. What an amazing man my husband was, how he reflected the Lord! They had grown to love him deeply also and were grateful for his love and acceptance of them.

As the week came to a close we regretfully, but with peace, saw them off on the plane. We watched it roar down the runway then it receded into the clear morning sky until it could be seen no more.

As soon as we were back home after seeing them off at the airport I looked up a couple of verses which had been running through my mind for days. 'Joy for the spirit of heaviness.'

I knew that was in Isaiah 61. It followed the verses which had long been a favourite of mine. Jesus used these same words when He first began His ministry.

'The Lord has anointed me to bring good news. . .
He has sent me to bind up the broken hearted. . .
freedom for captives and release for the prisoners. . .
to comfort those that mourn and provide for those who grieve. . . .'

I had long ago realized this showed me that as a Christian it was my task to help others to find the release Jesus brought.

The following verses spoke to me so intimately now.

'To give to those who mourn. . .
joy and gladness instead of grief. . .
a song of praise instead of sorrow. . .
and God will be praised for what He has done'!!

How true this was. Joy had replaced my desolation; my inner healing was being completed. God is so good, He loved me enough to allow this to happen; to bring Tom once again into my life. I had known all through the years God loved me. He said it in His word and I believed it but now it was evident in a new and dramatic way. God loves EACH of us with an everlasting love and desires that we recognize this. I had hung on to this fact in the dark and dreary days; clung to it year after year and now I knew it in the blazing joy of reunion.

The other words in my mind for days were 'enlarge your tent'. Now where could that be found? I had to go to the concordance to locate it. It was also from Isaiah, chapter 54.

'Enlarge your tent;
spread wide the curtains of your tent(dwelling)'.

Then it went on to my amazement,

126

'Fear not, you shall not be put to shame,
you shall suffer no insult,
and have no cause to blush.
It is time to forget
the shame of your younger days. . .
once deserted and heart broken.'

I sat glued to my chair; how specifically God was speaking to me! He was touching the depths of my spirit with the exactness of His word. But it went on, in the words of another translation, I had written in the margin years before.

'ALL your children will be taught of the Lord and great will be the peace of them.'

How precise and loving He is in His dealings with us. The Lord was giving me some very clear words of comfort and guidance and emphasizing to me again that He was in absolute control and working out this entire situation.

I wanted to mark this place so I reached into my Bible to pull out one of the innumerable bits of paper kept there. This just happened to be a piece of paper with a verse on it written by one of my fellow counsellors at 100 Huntley Street. She had given it to me in the early spring, long before things began happening. She said then that God gave her that particular verse, for me. It meant nothing to me at the time and I put it in my Bible and forgot all about it.

Now it did mean something!

'The blessing of the Lord makes rich
and there is no sorrow in it.'

God's voice was coming to me loud and clear. My heart was overwhelmed by joy and thankfulness. I immediately sensed that this blessing would be for more than just our immediate family. God's love and goodness toward us would bless others also. He seemed to stamp that clearly upon my heart.

It hardly seemed possible, just over two months ago I hadn't even known my son was alive and now we had met and begun to know each other. What joy! We must let go of our ordinary life, the four of us. 'Enlarge your tent' – our horizons were suddenly expanded. Our way of life had to be changed now that we had been given a whole new family to love and enfold in our lives.

I felt emotionally exhausted but blissfully happy, I would never be the same again. The prophet Joel in the Old Testament, expressed what God was doing in my life, 'He will give back the years the locusts have eaten.' God would make up the time that had been lost between us.

I praised God that He used my brokenness so I could hear Him more clearly and keep close to Him. I had known it was only He who could take away the pain. God doesn't make mistakes. The difficult, painful years had done positive things deep down in my life.

I had remarked in a letter to Tom a few weeks previously, 'I feel gritty, like someone who has been put into a rock tumbler and is being polished because of all that is happening to me.'

God tells us He wants to transform us into precious stones, jewels. He will use experiences in our lives to accomplish this. I had been through a painful polishing by the events swirling around me.

It reminded me of what someone had told me long before; God wraps each event in our lives with love and forgiveness. He transforms it into a jewel in His hands. I could feel He had been doing that with the grief and pain in my life. It was no longer a heavy ugly rock of sorrow; it had been transformed into a jewel of joy.

12: Sharing Our Joy

I will restore for you
the years that the locust has eaten. . .
. . . praise the name of the Lord your God
who has dealt wondrously with you.
Joel 2:25–26 (Amplified Bible)

We do not know what to do,
but we look to you for help.
2 Chronicles 20:12

How we yearned to share this news with our teenagers.
But we had to wait; Jean was still working at camp for
another couple of weeks and Andrew was in Alaska with
a missions team and wouldn't be back for a month. We
would tell them when we could all be together, but how
could we wait so long to share this wonderful news? I
wished those days away as until our children knew, we
did not feel free to share it with everyone else.

There had been just five friends the Lord had indi-
cated we should tell and we had done so; we needed
some friends to uphold us in prayer. The days until both
our teenagers returned dragged by as I was eager for
them to share our joyous news and enter into new
relationships with their unknown brother.

It was the end of August before we were finally all
together again. I looked around the supper table at the
other three, all in their usual places. Eric, across from
me at the head of the table looked towards me with a
reassuring smile, for he knew how difficult this was going
to be for me. He was my strength when I needed it; I

knew now he was praying we would share this news in a sensitive way.

On either side of me were our children, but children no more. Andrew had carried a man's responsibility all summer working on maintenance at a mission in Alaska. His dark curly head was bent as he finished the last of his supper.

'Lord don't let him be hurt,' I prayed silently, 'if only he can be reassured and know my love for him hasn't changed. He has always been so special to me; I had delighted in him and his quickness from the first. He was quick to laugh and absorb new things and show concern for others. Help him accept this news.'

I looked over to my left, and realized once again how much Jean resembled her brother. Where was my little girl with her long blonde hair? She was grown now into a lovely young lady with brown curly locks.

So alike in other ways, they were bright and alert, with happy gentle spirits. I was reminded that I didn't tell them often enough how much I loved them; they knew it but I felt I should put it into words more often. 'Thank you Lord for the joy they've given us and for the peace between them. I know it's your gift.' I sent up a silent prayer of thanks as I looked at them.

'Andrew and Jean we have something important to tell you,' Eric began, 'don't worry, it's good news. We want to tell you a story, a true story, that has a lot of sadness in it, but as you'll see it also has a lot of joy. It's a story of God at work in our lives.

'A long time ago before I ever met your mother, she had a baby who had to be given up for adoption.' There was complete silence and Eric continued.

'It's impossible to imagine the hurt that this caused her over the years. No-one knew about this. Even I knew nothing.'

He looked at three serious faces and said to me, 'Do you want to carry on?'

With a trembling voice I began. 'I had a phone call one afternoon from a social worker in Minneapolis who asked me some questions about my name and so on and then told me that my son wanted to get in touch with me.'

The details were then added, and Eric came around the table and put his arms around my shoulders. My tears were there at this point and as they flowed I managed to say.

'It's alright, these are happy tears at having Tom brought back to me.'

Eric added, 'You see the story is about God's love and forgiveness and restoration. We have prayed that you two will find out for yourselves that this will be a source of happiness when you take it all in. It is an awful lot for you to deal with all at once. After all it's not something that happens every day!'

I could see the looks of disbelief on their faces; they wondered if they were hearing correctly. So I said. 'I'm sorry this is such startling news. I know how hard it was for *me* to take it all in too. It took a long time.'

'It is just hard to believe. It doesn't seem real,' Andrew remarked.

Jean came over and put her arm around me as well and had tears in her eyes too.

'Dear, I know it is difficult for you both to have this come so suddenly.'

We hugged and I said again, 'Let me know if you have any questions and don't worry if it's hard to believe. I'm still overcome when I think about it.

'You know Tom is so eager to meet you, his new brother and sister. Here are some pictures we took when they were here.'

We looked at the photos we had taken on the momentous visit in July and filled in more of the details.

'One thing I kept saying when they were with us was, "if only Andrew and Jean could be here!" You'll enjoy knowing them.'

Over the next few days we talked more about the startling new events and they found themselves, like I was, still in a state of shock and disbelief. They said it was almost like it was happening to someone else.

Tom phoned them a couple of days later.

'I'm so thrilled to know I have another brother and sister. It would have been great to have met you both in July when we came to Toronto. But I hope it won't be too long until we do meet.

'I'm sorry this must all be such a surprise to you' Tom said.

'It is, but we are glad to hear about you and we have been looking at the pictures. Even so, it is hard to believe.'

Tom went on, 'I just hope my coming into your lives won't cause you any hurt or disruption. You're very special to me.'

The process of becoming acquainted was begun through letters and many more phone calls over the following weeks. There was a dramatic increase in our long distance phone bill, but it was worth every cent. I found increasing difficulty getting any time to talk with Tom myself!

Each time they talked I could see the animation in their faces; it told the real story of the beginning of this brand new relationship. We saw our two begin to experience the same joy and delight Eric and I had in knowing Tom and his family. We knew the two fellows would enjoy working together on cars. They shared other similar interests too such as a love of animals and the outdoors.

It was a delight at last to be free to speak of this wonderful news of God's restoration with our friends. We watched with amazement the same reaction in almost everyone as the tears welled up. They too could sense the hand of God in a unique way in this whole situation and the great joy it had brought to us. Indeed, just as the verse from Isaiah had pointed out, I felt no shame telling of all these events.

From first becoming a Christian I had known total forgiveness. I never carried a burden of guilt as I accepted the gift of forgiveness Jesus had offered me. Not to take it would have meant I was too proud.

Years ago I realized I had no reputation to defend; Christ 'made himself of no reputation'.* I had nothing to hold on to to make me worthwhile; my value was not in myself or my past, good or bad. God loved me and had forgiven me; that alone gave me worth.

As I shared my experiences of our reunion I was brought in touch with others who told me of their own painful experiences of having to give a child up in the past. Many had suffered great condemnation for all of this and found it hard to believe Jesus really forgave them, absolutely and completely. It was good to pray with them and see release. Some said it was the first time they had met another Christian who understood what they had been through and the grief they still carried.

When Tom was visiting us in the summer he met Don Osborne, in charge of the counselling ministry of the television programme, 100 Huntley Street. Don was as excited as we were with our reunion. Three months later, he asked if Eric and I would come on the programme, as guests, and share what God had been doing in our lives. He thought others should know the wonder of this restoration.

This confirmed a feeling I had had last summer. As soon as Tom and JoAnne left to go back home the Lord seemed to impress upon me that this whole experience was to be a blessing for more than just our own family. This was absolutely opposite my natural inclination.

These sort of 'feelings' need to be viewed critically and I don't respond impulsively to all impressions, but test them and hold them up to the light of Scripture. I was reminded of the verse, 'tell them what the Lord in His mercy has done for you.'*

I wanted Tom to go on the programme too and knew that if this was from the Lord the way would open up, but it didn't seem possible. The barrier was the cost of a flight from Phoenix to Toronto. The impression that Tom should come wouldn't leave and I told Eric, but no one else. We prayed that if Tom should be on the programme, then somehow it would be possible.

Just over a week before the broadcast in November a friend spoke to me.

'Is Tom coming up for the programme?'

'No he can't.'

'Why not?'

'It's too expensive. Neither of us can afford it right now.'

'Well, we feel it would make a real difference if Tom could tell his side of the story and *we* want to pay his way to come, subject to one condition.'

'What is that?'

'That no one knows who has done this.'

My response was instant. 'Yes. You know I have been praying for this and Tom's desire is to be here also. Thank you for being sensitive to what the Lord wanted you to do.'

This was an amazing offer; how marvellous to stand back and watch the Lord at work. It makes life exciting!

We phoned Tom and told him the good news and he was delighted. The arrangements were completed and he arrived late the evening before the scheduled broadcast. Once again he was flying into Toronto to see new relatives, not myself this time, but Andrew and Jean. This would be their first chance to meet.

There was excitement again as we drove out to the airport. Jean admitted to being slightly nervous but that was normal in the circumstances. It's not everyday one meets a new brother! Andrew as usual, took it more in his stride.

We had a good laugh together as we saw Tom appear, wearing a big cowboy hat.

'You know I like to travel comfortably!' He smiled and then there were hugs again for all of us.

Jean whispered to me, 'He doesn't look like his pictures, but much nicer!'

Once again we knew the oneness the Lord gives. We were all at ease in each other's company from the start and chatted away like old friends, in the car, after we got home and late into the night.

'I know it's not polite to stare,' Tom said, 'but I don't want to stop looking at you two. It's so good to see you and be with you.'

Eric turned to me and a smile covered his face.

'What are you smiling at?'

'You!'

'Why?' I asked.

'Just remembering all that's happened the last few months and knowing how you are feeling right now with all your children together!'

'Sweetheart, you have been through so much with me.'

My mind went back to the many ordinary tiring days, ones of heartache when the children were ill, and the many quiet evenings we had spent together. Love is woven from many different threads into the fabric of an enduring marriage.

'Eric, I was thinking about the verse the Lord gave us before we came to Canada.'

'Yes, you mean, "He will give us the desires of our heart" '?

'That's the one, but it reminded me of what you have often said. The desire of your heart was to be the best husband you could be. Now I see He has given you this. You have been all I needed especially in these past few hectic months. I could not have asked for anyone better.'

Next morning we went to the studio early to pray and get ourselves prepared for the programme. For days I had been praying to be sensitive to what the Lord wanted to be shared, not just what I felt was the right thing. There were a lot of people who would be watching who needed encouragement to believe God loved them and that He was capable of doing the impossible in their own particular situations.

As the programme progressed we felt relaxed and at ease. It seemed as if we were sitting around chatting with friends. How nice Don Osborne, whom we knew, could be taking the programme that day. It was a privilege to let others know they could trust God to do 'abundantly more than they could ask or think' when they trusted their lives to Him who loved them.*

It has been a source of pleasure to find out about the people this programme touched. Right in the studio audience there was a lady who had given up a child eight years before. We spoke after and I encouraged her to trust her daughter into God's care and pray for her.

I also received some very poignant letters from other birthmothers, telling of years of grief at the giving up of a child. They had never known any others who had done this and had found healing through the programme. They were impressed by Eric's loving support of me through it all; that he totally accepted all that had happened and still loved me.

The few hours we had with Tom came to an end all too soon. He and Andrew worked on the car. Tom had been thoughtful enough to bring a part he knew was needed for Andrew's car and helped him put it on. They both loved to fix things, especially cars.

When we took him to the plane our goodbyes were softened because in just three weeks we would be flying to Arizona for Christmas. We were looking forward to meeting Tom's parents and his three sisters. This would be moving into new territory for there are no guidelines for such meetings but we were anticipating it with pleasure. I wasn't concerned, his mom and dad had supported Tom in his search for me.

The 18th December rolled around quickly and school exams had come and gone. Christmas preparations were completed and we were off on our trip south.

Tom and JoAnne stood waiting for us and gave us more hugs. Jean soon saw she was the smallest of the 'little' people.

'Where are Josh and Troy?' we asked, looking around.

'We left them at home, Troy needs his nap, and it's easier to visit at the beginning without them. We're

taking you out for lunch to one of our favourite spots.'
JoAnne said.

We walked along, arm in arm, JoAnne was walking
with Eric and teasing him again.

'I think you love him as much as I do Jo'

'Maybe. He's a great fellow, even if he is short!'

'Remember,' Eric laughed, 'good things come in small
packages.'

We went for a leisurely lunch, at ease and enjoying
the special company we were with. How good it was to
be together!

We had a guided tour on the way back to Tom's
house.

'Aren't those lovely oranges,' I said seeing the street
lined with orange trees heavy with fruit.

'I'm afraid those are inedible, they're purely orna-
mental and too sour to eat. We have some back in our
garden as well as peach and grapefruit trees. You can
have a taste of the grapefruit, they're almost ready.'

'It seems funny to see people in down winter jackets
with it a warm 60 degrees.' Andrew remarked.

'Guess they would freeze to death up in Toronto if
they have to bundle up so much here.' Jean said.

'Look! Palm trees like there were in Kenya.'

'Those are date palms and over there are royal palms,
we have five types down here. Tomorrow, when Jo has
to work, I'll take you to the Desert Museum. They have
1500 varieties of cactus and desert plants there.'

'I remember that place, it's great. I saw it when I was
here two years ago with a friend.' Andrew said.

'We didn't know who lived here then.'

We all laughed knowing the special tie we had. We
spent most of the next ten days together in relaxed enjoyment of each others' company.

That first evening we met Tom's parents and his
sisters. I was able to give them a hug and my thanks in
person.

'It's special to meet you and to see the family Tom
has belonged to all these years. I feel so grateful for your

care of him. It means a lot to be able to have this chance to get to know you. I must say I think you have done a wonderful job raising him!'

'He's a great fellow. We are pleased with him, but then we had good material to work with!', they said. Tom seemed a bit overcome by all the attention.

'Thank you for helping and encouraging Tom in his search for me.'

'We knew it meant a lot to him and we just felt it would be good whatever he found and that he would be happy finding you.'

We all knew how true it was and how it had enhanced the relationship Tom had with his family.

It was interesting to know Mrs. Rye was also a nurse and we had some 'shop talk'. While we were there we attended the graduation of Tom's oldest sister, Kathy, who had just become a nurse. Tom's younger sisters, Barb and Nancy, were also working in hospitals as well.

We had a busy few days sightseeing and talking before Christmas. There were many new things to see and places to go; we even went down into Mexico for the day. Later Tom showed us his large desert tortoises which mowed his grass very effectively. We gradually learned the names of many different desert plants.

Christmas morning at Tom's and we exchanged gifts; this was the first time we could give a tangible expression of the love we felt. We had all taken special thought and care in choosing or making these gifts.

'Tom here is a reminder of me and of Canada. It's a sweater for you made from wool which I dyed and spun. These deep purple colours are from lichen dyes and the dark brown and other shades are just the natural colour of the wool. I hope you like it.'

'Thank you Nancy, that's special,' Tom said as he gave me a hug. 'I'll always remember this first Christmas we had together.'

'It's nice to be able to make you something because I've made many things for Andrew and Jean over the years. This will be my most memorable Christmas ever. I've been given the best gift of all this year, YOU!'

We enjoyed Christmas dinner with the Ryes; there were over thirty friends and relations gathered at Tom's parents. They were a bit concerned and his dad asked me, 'Nancy, I hope it's not too overwhelming having this many people around?'

'Oh no, we're enjoying it; it's good to meet more of your family and see how Tom fits into it all. How grand to acquire all these new friends and relations. We have never had a lot of family close by, so it's delightful.'

As we were talking later Tom's mother said, 'You know I keep feeling I've seen you somewhere before Nancy.'

I laughed; 'You have. You've been looking at me for 27 years!'

After the holidays we did more travelling, up into northern Arizona, in the mountains where we even saw snow. Most of the time it was rather cold and rainy. We spent time out on the hillside looking at rocks and found some interesting bits of petrified wood. Perhaps we were crazy to be out in the cold but we had fun doing it. We were excited to be discovering the hand of God in the great diversity of rocks and plants.

Tom and JoAnne, Andrew and Jean all enjoyed each other's company in spite of the differences in ages. I was intrigued by the similarities; the same laughing eyes, the tender heart and gentleness.

The two younger members of the family, Tom's sons, Joshua and Troy, gave us a great deal of pleasure and it was a new experience for Andrew and Jean as they don't have many relatives that young.

Later, Tom and I were talking.

'Tom you are so like my other two in many ways and like myself but I can see danger areas where you also are like me, and shouldn't be. You can get so busy and not spend enough time with your family; you try and do too much! Be careful, take time to cultivate the good relationship with JoAnne and the kids.'

'Yes I do realize that too and try to watch it carefully because I love them so much.'

'I can see you do and that's wonderful, but being too busy probably also carries over into neglecting time with the Lord, doesn't it? You see I know myself.'

Tom laughed, 'Yes, we are alike in bad ways too.'

We went out for our last meal together; it had been a good ten days. We sat around the table enjoying the good Mexican food. We sensed a deep bond and it seemed we all fitted together as though we had always been around each other.

'It has meant so much to me to have found you Nancy. I feel like I finally found myself, when I found my roots, my background. I always felt as though I had no history of my own, and that my past was a big blank. It leaves one with an empty feeling; because something is missing.'

'Tom, I was wrong when I wrote, in my first letter, that the past wasn't important. I didn't realize that it was to you. I was wondering if you had tried to trace your father yet?'

'No I haven't but now I feel like I can get on with life in a new way. It is a new kind of security knowing what my past is, and knowing you.'

'Remember we talked another time about one of Paul Tournier's books, *A Place for You*?'

'Yes, I remember.'

'He says we all seek for a place, especially like you when you were torn up from your roots. He said we all seek not just our roots, our place in this world but our place before God.'

'That's what they were saying on the 100 Huntley Street programme when we were on wasn't it?'

'Yes, remember they talked about when we find the Lord we find out who we are and that fills a deep longing in us.'

'When I came to know Jesus it was a wonderful sense of knowing He loved me and now when my search was completed and I found you. . .' Tom was at a loss for words. He went on, 'but in a wonderful way I feel closer to my adoptive family because of it all. I think we have even a deeper relationship now than ever before.'

I reached across the table and put my hand over his, 'I'm glad, that's the way it should be. God's love never takes away, it only makes things better.'

We looked over at the others laughing and chatting. 'It's been so good to get acquainted with Andrew and Jean, I love them so much, they are very special people, Eric too.'

'They are, but you know it's not a matter of getting acquainted for us two, rather it's just the fact of being able to be together. It's hard to put into words.'

'Our friendship is a special gift from the Lord,' Tom replied.

Goodbyes the next day were extremely difficult, maybe it was because the Lord had knit us so close to one another. We knew we had to go; we each had our own lives to live but there was now an added dimension to them. We wished there weren't so many miles between us. But there had to be a letting go, our children have lives of their own. We can look ahead with thankfulness for all the years ahead of us.

After our return home I sat one evening thinking of all that had transpired, when Eric spoke;

'Nan, remember the poem, *Rabbi Ben Ezra*, by Browning? I've often quoted it!

'Is that the one you used to mention in your letters?'

'Yes. Its fitting for us now. It goes like this,

'Grow old along with me!
The best is yet to be,
The last of life
for which the first was made:
Our times are in His hand
Who saith, "A whole I planned
Youth shows but half;
Trust God: see all,
Nor be afraid." '

s.c.—8

Conclusion

As the Father has loved me,
so I have loved you.
Dwell in my love.
If you heed my commands,
you will dwell in my love.
I have spoken thus to you,
so that my joy may be in you,
and your joy complete.
John 15:9–11

Overwhelming victory is ours
through Him who loves us.
For I am convinced that there is
nothing in death or life
or in the realm of spirits
or superhuman powers,
in the world as it is
or the world as it shall be,
in the forces of the universe,
in heights or depths
– NOTHING in all creation
that can separate us from the love of God
in Christ Jesus our Lord.
Romans 8:39

Down through the years the joy in my life was often only a tiny, flickering flame in the darkness; at times it shone brighter. Now it has been blown upon by the Spirit of God into a blazing fire in my heart. My son which was lost is found. I have been overwhelmed by joy.

But where do I, we, go from here? Life will never be the same again. God has taken hold of my life; taken the traumatic events and transformed them into undreamed of joy.

These recent events have caused me to stand in awe as I see God's love and His sovereignty. I knew this before but now it is inscribed on my heart. God loves me. He is in control of everything.* He is able to do far more than I could ask or think. He wants to bring me into an increasingly deeper, trusting walk with Himself.

My Christian life is not made up of saying some words, but a lifetime of fellowship with the Risen Christ. It is not a matter of how well or often I pray, or how many things I can do for Him. It is learning to love Him with my whole heart, soul and mind.

Neither is my relationship with Tom a matter of words; legally he is no longer my son. But he chose to come back into contact with me and now we have a loving relationship that will grow richer over the years. We are bonded close, and yet it will only enhance the relationship he has with his adopted family. A lifetime of shared experiences with them has produced the deep love which he has for his parents and sisters. I can never take their place, nor do I want to.

Often in life we find ourselves faced with impossible choices, none of which seems good. Still some decision must be made. My decision to allow Tom's adoption produced hurt far beyond my comprehension. And yet I felt there was no alternative, any other choice would have caused even greater trouble in Tom's life. At least this way I, not he, could carry the burden.

Sometimes our choice is only between different types of pain. Love may be keeping a child but it may be loving the child enough to see they have a normal healthy family life. Loving can be caring more for them than our own immediate gratification.

I am thankful my pain caused me to love God, seek after Him and not become bitter. What happens to us is really not the important thing but how we respond to it. Over the years I've had to root out bitterness, anger and resentment. It was a deliberate choosing to reject those; a choosing to live again and not focus on my problems. I had to focus on Jesus and not the 'what ifs'.

The traumatic events in our lives can set the stage for glorious new beginnings if we have real repentance, not merely a feeling sorry for ourselves. Suffering is universal, we all carry some sort; others have a different type from mine but it's equally painful. The Lord is able to bring us through all of it with victory if we cooperate with Him.*

Part of this involves letting go of the past, or it becomes a heavy stone, dragging us down. I had to choose the way of forgiveness and joy, and to cultivate it by a deliberate choice. I often failed to do this but had to try again; each time it became a bit easier.

That didn't mean I didn't have feelings of anger or fear; it only caused more problems later if I covered these up and pretended they were not there. It was necessary to acknowledge my grief and agony to myself and to the Lord. Healing from these takes time but, in Christ, God's love comes to us to meet our every need.

When my father left us I was too young to recognize my devastation and my feelings of rejection from this experience, although they were there. Now I have to recognize my hurt and allow God to mend it and be willing to let go of anger or resentment.

Many people in similar situations feel that God will not want to use them but that is not true, for He does not just use perfect people.* We can be used and discarded by others but God never rejects us and wants to use us even in our brokenness to touch others. Life must go on and we realize no one is completely whole but only in the process of becoming.

Year by year I have sensed God's love in a deeper way and exposed my wounds for Him to heal.* The walls I erected around my heart, to shield and protect it, have come down. This makes me much more vulnerable and I can and have been hurt afresh more easily. That is the risk I have to take to keep living and loving His way. Others have failed me but I must choose to trust again. His love draws me to want to be more like Him.

There is always something new in life; God has an individual, loving plan for each of us which makes life a great adventure.* We just need to be open to His directing. He makes me want to learn to love Him with a child-like freshness; recklessly, extravagantly.

Not only has the sovereignty of God and His love for us become real to me in a new way I've also seen the emphasis He has put on adoption and restoration.

Love and restoration are at the heart of all God's dealings with us. He wants us brought into fellowship with Him; to come back where we belong and become what He wants us to be. When I do that I find the real freedom in the total forgiveness He offers.* The Lord knows me completely and yet loves me absolutely.*

The Bible tells me, 'He will restore the years the locust have eaten',* that means the years Tom and I have lost will be restored to us. We can't, in reality, have the actual years back but He will make it up in new and wonderful ways. For this to happen we both have to co-operate and not look back with regret but enjoy what is ahead of us.

Through our reunion I have been made aware how close to the heart of God is the whole idea of adoption; it is referred to throughout Scripture. When we enter into a personal relationship with Christ He tells us we are adopted into His family. We become His children purchased at great price by the blood Christ shed. He assures us that we are His and causes us to cry, 'Abba, Father, Daddy'.*

God has shown He specifically used adopted people for important tasks; Moses was adopted by Pharaoh's daughter and in that way was prepared for the ministry God had for him. Esther, adopted by her uncle Mordecai, found herself in the place God wanted her to be so that she too could be used by Him.*

I know God has allowed Tom and me to be moulded

by the events of our lives to prepare us for what He wants done. He does not waste lives or events but transforms for good.

Adoptive parents don't have to fear that their child will stop loving them if there should ever by a reunion with a birth parent. From our own situation and talking with many others it seems the adoptive family is drawn closer together through a reunion.

Parents fear their children will grow away from them but in all growing up there is a growing away and this is normal. Our children must become persons in their own right and we must help them to do so. When we can do this together we remain close as a family.

The Lord needs adoptive parents and I praise God there are special people like Glen and Nita Rye. They cared for my child when I, who was in an impossible situation, couldn't. From my hurt could come joy for them and now I share it too.

They were also sensitive enough to see that I might long for news of my son and they helped Tom in his search and have been rewarded by becoming closer as a family. I hope this will encourage others.

Adoption should not be a purely legal transaction, with its absolute severing of relations but should somehow rather be on-going. It should meet the needs of everyone; adoptive parents, the child and the birth parents. The adopted child may have a desire to know his roots or to reassure their birth mother that they are being well cared for and loved. What a comfort it would be for her to know that. This contact could be done, with privacy guaranteed and progress reported upon over the years.

Birth mothers could let their child know how they loved them and provide the genetic and medical background they may need. In certain circumstances this medical information can be of vital importance, even a matter of life and death. If there are hereditary diseases the adoptive family should know or the child's life could be in jeopardy.

Some adopted people may want to have a reunion when they are adult enough to handle all that is involved. Tom said how glad he was to have waited until he was mature enough to cope with all the intense emotions.

Perhaps for many it will take time for them to even acknowledge the hurt and anger buried inside them as they feel so rejected. 'Why was I given up?' They must come to grips with this and allow God to heal it.

I still see areas that are very puzzling and difficult. Is search and contact right for everyone? I don't know. I can imagine there are cases where a lost child turning up after many years could cause a shaky marriage to fall apart. But if the adoptee is caring and if the search is carried out with great responsibility and sensitivity, problems will be avoided.

Tom did his search in this way and respected my right to privacy. He didn't barge in uninvited, he asked gently, through a third party, for contact with me. He understood and accepted, no matter how hard it was at the time, my reluctance for full and open contact at first. It takes time to come to accept news as startling and far reaching in its consequences as this.

I had also to be sensitive to Tom's need to have contact and information and take the risk of allowing him into our lives. If I had allowed fear to rule my life I would not have experienced the healing joy that reunion brought.

Professional help, as we had, is useful in these emotionally stressful situations to guide everyone through contact and reunion. Far too often there is unfounded fear of what will happen.

Apparently, from reports of hundreds of contacts I've read and heard about, any contact and information is important for adoptees. Any information about their roots is a very healing thing even when there is not a very good reunion. Our reunion may be the exception rather than the rule but if the situation is placed in God's hands it must bring good. Even with a less than satisfactory outcome it is immeasurably appreciated as the void of the past is filled in.

Can there be some alternative to current adoption practices? I don't know. I'm not sure that a teenage, single mother keeping her child is usually healthy for either but some do it successfully. If they do keep their child they need lots of loving support. If a birth mother knew there would not be an absolute severing; if she could have some news, maybe more babies might be available to be raised with loving, stable, adoptive parents.

Something must be done to bring inner healing to those involved in adoption. Some counselling services report 40–50% of their clients are adoptees! Is this not a cry for help? Many have a deep sense of betrayal. They have a deep longing to FEEL really loved. Only the Lord can give this.

Abortion is certainly NOT the answer. God has formed that new life and it is not our right to kill. Psalm 139 states that God formed us in our mother's womb. Jeremiah also echoes the care and purpose God has for us even before He forms us, pre-natally. He has a purpose for each child that is conceived. It is very hard to go through a pregnancy but with support it can be done.

For those who may have gone through the trauma of an abortion may I suggest you might use the prayer I've included in the appendix.

How can we help unwed mothers in a situation like mine? First there must be an acceptance of them as a person; God loves them even though He does not condone sin; for He knows the grief it brings. I feel God doesn't have any different grades of sin, some worse than others; theirs is a visible sin, ours may not be.

Is the Lord not asking the Church and us as individuals in it to show love, compassion, and practical help to the unwed mothers in our midst? We must be a haven for them whether they decide to keep their child or not.

Studies have shown adopted children so often have deep feelings of loneliness and rejection which have come during pregnancy or after. These need healing and it probably doesn't have to be done in person, that is the better way I'm sure.

Both sets of parents could pray for their child. Perhaps the prayer from the appendix could be used as a guide. We need to come in faith knowing He is able and will do more than we can ask or think.

I am still very puzzled why some have such difficulty accepting God's total and complete forgiveness.* Why do we listen to lies like, 'God can't love you. Look what you have done'. Once we confess our sin to God, we are forgiven and He forgets all about it. To not accept His forgiveness is to mock God. His love is totally unmerited and enough to cover all my sin.

We are precious to Him, God says to us 'I LOVE YOU.' The cross stands forever as a sign and seal of His love.* In the relinquishment of a child there is a mixture of both grief and guilt. He totally forgives; our past is covered and He desires to transform it into something beautiful.

God doesn't ask us to pay for our former lifestyles; Jesus did that. Granted we may bear the sorrow of them but He wants to help do that as well.

At the same time I also have the responsibility to pray for anyone my actions may have harmed. My way of life must change, I must go God's way and obey Him. This relationship with Him must be cultivated, like any other, by communication in prayer and His word. There is a need to learn from other mature Christians and reach out and serve others.

Keeping the secret of my child's existence from Eric was difficult. I longed to share it with him and perhaps should have done so; but with circumstances being what they were, I didn't and then my desire to avoid causing any hurt sealed my lips.

I have found how satisfying it is in the arms of God; there is a shallowness about everything else. The Lord wants to deal with our emptiness and deep hurts and fill the void inside. We must let Him have the freedom to touch our lives. Frances Roberts in her book, *Come Away My Beloved*, says this very beautifully.

'Behold with great love I have chosen thee and made thee Mine, saith the Lord. . . I wait for thee to turn from everything else to Me alone. I want you to give Me all of yourself. I want the real you. The more you can bring to Me of your true self, the more I can give to you of My true self. . .

I come to thee via my Holy Spirit from depths within thy being that thou hast never plumbed; from chambers within thy soul which thine eyes have never seen.*

Rooms of darkness.

Not dark because of sin necessarily, as ye think of sin; but dark because they have been kept closed.

Indeed, none but I have the key to open them. I not only have the power to open them, but the wisdom and the love; and I never confront thee with that which I do not give thee grace to meet'!!

As I look at myself and back at my past it is the truth as I can perceive it, and as I saw and felt it. But so much remains a mystery. Only *after* Tom found me did I see the full depth of my grief which I had carried all these years. So much was hidden before, even from myself.

Each day is a new beginning, we are not bound by the past.* I have to respect myself in spite of all my faults and things that still need changing. God isn't finished with me yet! He loves me and stimulates me to change. He wants us to have His presence and the power of the Holy Spirit so we might go through life with His victory.

God has mended the broken pieces of my life and transformed them in ways undreamed of. I am now able to praise Him for that which once caused such pain.* 'It was intended for harm but God used it for good.'* He transformed the void of grief to overflowing joy.

Praise His Name.

'. . . forgetting what is behind me, and reaching out for that which lies ahead, I press towards the goal to win the prize which is God's call to the life above, in Christ Jesus.' Philippians 3:13

Prayers, Scripture References and Helpful Books

Prayer for Adoptive Parents

Lord Jesus we come with this your child. We thank you for giving him/her to us, thank you for all the joys and sorrows that this has brought. We know they are ours as a 'trust' that we might provide what could not have been given any other way. We are glad you chose us to be . . . 's family.

Your word tells us you have formed us in our mother's womb and for your own. You wanted . . . even when others didn't in difficult circumstances. We forgive those who have seemed to fail us and who left us in our early days. So in the Name of Jesus we stand against the spirit of rejection and accept your total acceptance of us.

You were always right there with . . . for you have told us 'you will never leave us or forsake us'. You have been with us every moment of every day even though we didn't know it.

We also want to break any ties with the occult or that which is not of God, In the Name of Jesus Christ. We ask You to break all harmful genetic ties and create in . . . all the fullness of the Lord himself.

We bring our child to you Lord and ask again for you to care for them, . . . is yours. Give us your love, your wisdom and power to help them to become all you want them to be. We ask that they will grow to love you more and praise you, who alone are worthy.

Jeremiah 1:4–5

Prayer for Adopted Children

I love you Lord and come to you in my need. Thank you that you brought me into being, that you wanted ME. You have told me I am precious in your sight and I accept that. You formed me in my mother's womb, You caused me to grow and develop. You wanted me when others didn't or couldn't.

I determine to forgive all those who have hurt me or wronged and failed me. Bring to mind anyone I need to forgive. (Pause and name each one). I forgive . . . because You have forgiven me.

I come against the spirits of rejection and loneliness which were with me before I knew anything. I accept the fact you were always with me Jesus. I was never rejected by You. 'You will never leave me or forsake me.' Praise you Lord, You were with me and loved me when others didn't.

I offer to You all the hurts of my life; I give them to You as an offering. I refuse to hold on to them any longer. Forgive me for the resentment and anger I feel towards . . . Forgive me where I have failed You.

I accept your total and complete forgiveness and release; I am free in you to be the person you want me to be.

Thank you for the assurance that you love me and 'rejoice over me like a bridegroom rejoices over his bride.' I am precious to you.

I believe 'You have chosen me and I have no cause to fear, You will be with me; You are my God and will strengthen me and help me and support me with YOUR hand.'

I give You my adoptive family and thank you for providing me a family to care for me. Bless them and my birth family.

I give myself to You, use me for Your glory.

Jeremiah 1:4–5; Isaiah 62:6; Isaiah 41:10

Prayer for Birth Parents

I come to You Heavenly Father and thank You for Your love that has been with me all the years of my life. Thank you Jesus that in Your death I am forgiven and free.

I give you the burden and grief of my child I released for adoption. Forgive my sin that allowed this child to have to be separated from me. I receive your forgiveness for you have said 'when I confess my sins You are faithful and just and You forgive all my sins.'

Touch my emptiness, my sorrow, I give them to You to bear for me. Take this heavy load of grief and I receive Your Holy Spirit to minister to my deep needs.

I forgive those who have hurt me and used me (name each one). I release them to Your hands.

I also place my child into Your care, protect him/her, love them as only You can. Help them to know my love and Your love for them. Touch their hearts with peace.

I stand against any spirit of rejection which has come to them in our separation in Jesus' Name. Cause them to love you and to walk in Your ways.

I thank you for their adoptive parents and bless them. Give them Your wisdom, gentleness and love in raising our child.

Thank you that Your love for us never ceases and it will be new to me every morning. I take it as my strength and comfort and walk before You with new joy every day. Praise you Lord.

(1 John 1:9; Lamentations 3:22)

Prayer For Those Who Have Had an Abortion

Lord you know me and the child I once carried and which I allowed to be aborted. You alone know the pressures I was under from others and from my own selfishness. That child was an intrusion upon my life and I did not want it.

Forgive me Lord, I allowed my child's life to be taken.

It was you who were forming his/her life there inside me and I took that life.

Lord Jesus you love me just as I am but I know You want to forgive me. I have done what is wrong in your sight. Your word gives me the assurance that 'if I confess my sins You are just and can be trusted to forgive my sins and cleanse me from EVERY kind of wrong.'

Oh God, help me accept Your TOTAL forgiveness. I am made clean by the blood of the Lamb: I receive that. You have also said 'You will remember my sin no more.' Wipe my own memory clean and cause me to walk in newness of life. Cleanse my body, soul and spirit from all the effects of that abortion, in the Name of Jesus.

I forgive all who have wronged me (name each one). I release them into Your hands. I receive Your forgiveness and Your love and let them pour over me like a river. I forgive myself as you have forgiven me for 'there is no condemnation for those who are in Christ Jesus. He has set me free.'

I place that life that was within me into Your hands. Lord receive their spirit, they are now Yours. I know you love them.

I give to You all the guilt and anguish I have carried. Fill that void with yourself. I receive You Lord and the joy You will give me. Dwell in me and help me to dwell close to You.

I praise and worship You Lord, who alone are worthy.

(Jeremiah 1:4–5; 1 John 1:9; Isaiah 43:25; Romans 8:1–3)

Scripture References*

Chapter 1
page 14 Jeremiah 1:4–5; page 16 Jeremiah 29:11–14; page 18 Psalm 56:8.

Chapter 2
page 22 Isaiah 48:18; page 23 Romans 3:11,23–24; Eph 2:8–10; Hebrews 10:17; page 23 Romans 5:8; Isaiah 61:10; page 25 Luke 11:25.

Chapter 3
page 31 2 Timothy 2:15; page 31 Psalm 40:2; page 33 John 14.

Chapter 5
page 49 Ruth 1:16–17; page 54 Genesis 28:15.

Chapter 6
page 58 Isaiah 48:18; page 60 2 Corinthians 10:5; page 60 Romans 8:1; page 65 Jeremiah 29:12–13.

Chapter 7
page 70 Isaiah 49:15–16; page 74 Philippians 4:11.

Chapter 8
page 80 Isaiah 53:5; page 81 Luke 11:9–13; page 81 John 1:33; Luke 24:49; page 81 Colossians 2:7; page 81 John 14:15–16,26; page 83 Hebrews 10:24–25; page 83 1 Corinthians 2:9–10; page 83 Psalm 45:7; Psalm 23:5; page 84 Nehemiah 8:10.

Chapter 9
page 89 Philippians 3:13; page 94 Hebrews 13:5; page 94 Romans 12:12, 15:13, I Thessalonians 5:16–18; page 94 Psalm 22:3; page 95 Psalm 37:3–5,7; page 96 Philippians 3:10; page 96 Hebrews 13:8; page 96 Proverbs 17:22.

Chapter 10
page 103 Hebrews 13:5; page 103 Psalm 22:3; page 103 Romans 8:26–27; page 104 Jeremiah 1:4–5; page 107 Ephesians 5:22.

Chapter 11
page 117 Luke 15:23–24; page 117 Psalm 118:23; page 118 Psalm 68:6; page 128 Isaiah 49:18, 54:11.

Chapter 12
page 133 Philippians 2:7; page 133 Isaiah 12:4–6, Mark 5:19; page 136 Ephesians 3:20.

Chapter 13
page 143 Isaiah 45:5–7, 46:9–10; page 144 Romans 5:3; page 144 Isaiah 43:18,25; page 144 Isaiah 58:6; page 145 Matthew 11:28–30, Song of S 2:4; page 145 Jeremiah 1:4–5; page 145 Isaiah 58:6; page 145 Psalm 73:23–24; page 145 Joel 2:25–26; page 145 Romans 8:14–16; page 145 Exodus 2, Esther; page 149 Psalm 103:12; page 149 John 3:16; page 150 John 16:13; page 150 Lamentations 3:22–23; page 150 Romans 5:3; page 150 Genesis 50:20.

Helpful Books

It is good to learn from others. Over the years many authors have echoed my own searchings; either in what I had found or by what God was leading me into. They instilled in me a further hunger for a deeper experience of the Living Lord, who alone satisfies our longing heart.

Just a few of many:

Brother Lawrence, *The Practice of the Presence of God*,
. . . a 16th century monk who shows the delight of communing with God in whatever we are doing.

Catherine Marshall, *Something More*,
. . . the 'so much mores' of God, and of the need to forgive.

Paul Tournier, *A Place for You* and *Secrets*,
. . . a Swiss physician who clearly and practically shows the medicine of the whole person in the light of God's word.

C. S. Lewis, *Surprised by Joy* and other books,
. . . perhaps Christianity's greatest mind, tells of the joy in knowing Christ.

Frances Roberts, *Come Away My Beloved*,
. . . prophetic devotional readings which show the depth of God's love for us.

Rita Bennett, *Emotionally Free*,
. . . describes the liberation Christ can bring when He heals past hurts.

Betty Tapscott, *The Gift of Inner Healing*,
. . . another good book on inner healing.

Francis McNutt, *Healing*,
. . . a very comprehensive book on all aspects of inner healing.

Michael Harper, *Walking in the Spirit*,
. . . the first book I read on what it means to have a Spirit-filled life.

Watchman Nee, *Sit, Walk, Stand* and others,
. . . he consistently challenges us to all we are and have in the Lord.

Dean Merill, *Another Chance—How God Overrides Our Big Mistakes*,
. . . illustrates God's mercy and forgiveness.